Introduction to DECORATIVE PAINTING

Introduction —to— DECORATIVE PAINTING

Lea Davis

Kangaroo Press

This book, as always, is dedicated to the memory of
Colin Charlton (1956–1979).
Beloved brother, loved for all time.

Acknowledgments

Few things in this life are possible without the love and support of family and friends and I was truly blessed when the Lord chose mine.

Philip, my husband
Mike and Tim, my sons
Sue, Peter, Casey and Scottie, my family
Mum and Dad
Noel, my father-in-law
Carolyn Ballantine
Sylvia and Carol (deceased) from Craftee Cottage, Oakleigh
Sheila Cafferkey
John and Isabel Birch
Stan Clifford and all at DecoArt™
Cheryl Bradshaw
Bryce Dunkley

A special thank you to my students, my friends, who are always there to add support and encouragement. (You would think after all these years you would have learnt how to paint!):
Barb, Josie, Chris, Chrissie, Miriam, Val, Betty, Mary and Jeanette
Wilma, Verna, Jose, Renate, Lorraine, Jean, Maida and Suzanne.

All my friends at the Society of Folk and Decorative Artists of Victoria.
I would encourage all painters to join their local decorative painting society. The friends you make will last a lifetime.

If you have a moment to spare I would love to hear from you. My address is:

PO Box 3047 Murrumbeena Victoria 3163 Australia

INTRODUCTION TO DECORATIVE PAINTING
[The first edition of this book was titled *Introduction to Folk Art* (1992)]

This edition first published in Australia in 1999 by Kangaroo Press
an imprint of Simon & Schuster (Australia) Pty Limited
20 Barcoo Street, East Roseville NSW 2069

A Viacom Company
Sydney New York London Toronto Tokyo Singapore

© Lea Davis 1992 and 1999

All rights reserved. No part of this publication may be reproduced, stored in a retrieval system, or transmitted, in any form or by any means, electronic, mechanical, photocopying, recording or otherwise, without the prior permission of the publisher in writing.

National Library of Australia
Cataloguing-in-Publication data

Davis, Lea.
Introduction to decorative painting.

New ed.
Includes index.
ISBN 0 86417 953 7.

1. Folk art. 2. Decoration and ornament. 3. Painting - Technique. I. Davis, Lea. Introduction to folk art. II. Title. III. Title: Introduction to folk art.

745.723

Photographer: Bryce Dunkley

Set in Palatino 10/12
Printed in Singapore by Colour Symphony Pte Ltd

10 9 8 7 6 5 4 3 2 1

CONTENTS

Introduction 7
Materials and equipment 8
 • *Paints* • *Brushes* • *Caring for your brushes* • *Palette* • *Other equipment*
Surface preparation 11
 • *Wood* • *Metal*
Tracing and transferring a design 13
 • *Tracing the design* • *Transfer paper method* • *Chalk method*
Stroke formation 14
 • *Hand and body position* • *Loading and dressing the brush* • *Thinning the paint* • *Stroke formation with the round brush* • *Brush stroke worksheet* • *Stroke formation with the liner brush* • *Special brush techniques*
Background techniques 23
 • *Sponging* • *Faux finish with plastic wrap* • *Criss-cross background*
Antiquing 26
 • *Oil antiquing* • *Water-based antiquing* • *Selective antiquing* • *Gilding*
Finishing techniques 29
 • *Varnishing* • *Staining* • *Crackling*
THE PROJECTS
  Rocking horse 32
  Oval garland box 35
  Lap desk and pencil caddy set 37
  Garden set 41
  Faux finish coaster box with peonies 44
  Dinner cats 46
  Three papier-mâché daisy boxes 50
  Roses heart box 53
  Pansy teapot and sugar bowl 55
  Tissue box cover and picture frame 58
  Wildflower box 60
  Blue bowl 63
Patterns 67
Stockists 80
Index 80

INTRODUCTION

This book was written with the beginning folk artist/decorative painter in mind, and is meant as a starting point for your journey through this art form. There is so much that could be covered but to include too much would be overwhelming for the beginner, so I have included only the basic information. The patterns on the whole are simple, with a few more difficult pieces thrown in for inspiration (hopefully!). It is far better to paint a simple design well than to try something harder and get into difficulties. Don't be discouraged if your piece doesn't turn out as well as you had hoped. Decorative painting is not a perfect art.

If I could write three words that make you a better painter they would be —
PRACTICE, PRACTICE, PRACTICE.

How boring! you are probably saying, but each time you practise you are improving your skills, and in no time at all you will see the results for yourself. I still have the first sheet of comma strokes I ever painted, and I cringe each time I look at them — but I keep them to remind myself how I have improved. It's a great idea to keep, say, one sheet from each month as comparison.

I wish you luck as you begin your painterly journey and I know all those around you will benefit from your newly acquired skills.

In friendship,
Lea Davis

OPPOSITE: *This great little set, described on page 44, keeps your coasters all together. There are 8 coasters inside — I have gilded four and faux finished four. This is a quick and easy project and makes a great gift.*

MATERIALS & EQUIPMENT

PAINTS

I have taught my sons that you should start out how you mean to finish, so even though you are a beginner it is important to use only artist quality paints and mediums. You are creating tomorrow's antiques and the time and effort you are expending on each of your pieces deserves only the very best of products. Try not to be tempted by student quality paints—these for the most part are not the correct consistency for strokework, nor are they heavily pigmented or light-fast. Please do not use house paint.

I love to use DecoArt™ Americana paints because they are intermixable and suitable for use on most surfaces such as wood, tin, ceramics, paper, plaster and fabric (with the addition of a medium). There are many other wonderful brands on the market such as Matisse, Jo Sonja® and Delta Ceramcoat. These brands are all water-based, non-toxic, artist quality acrylic paints.

BRUSHES

The beginning artist has a vast array of brushes from which to choose and this task alone is enough to make all but the most enthusiastic beginners throw up their hands and forget the whole thing. For this reason, Francheville have packaged a beginner's set of Eco Fibre® brushes by Lea Davis. These brushes are perfect for the beginning Folk Artist with all the characteristics that are desirable in a brush—spring, flow control, durability and price—and I have chosen the sizes after careful consideration. The size 5 Eco Fibre® brush is perfect for larger flowers and leaves. The size 3 Eco Fibre® is easier to manage than the size 5, so use this when you are painting smaller flowers and leaves, etc.; 10/0 Eco Fibre® Liner brush is perfect for long thin lines, tendrils and stems. They can be used on all surfaces and in all paints and mediums and are particularly well suited for acrylic paints. Brushes are an integral part of your painting and while they are not part of your completed work, the type of brush you use is evident in the end result.

Other brushes

You will also need brushes for basecoating. Sponge brushes are inexpensive and are ideal for the beginner. They come in a range of sizes and a 50 mm (2") sponge brush is a good starting point.

As you become more proficient you may like to add a 25 mm (1") flat basecoating brush to your painting kit. These are expensive but help you achieve beautiful basecoats.

I also use a 25 mm (1") flat bristle brush for some of my background techniques. These are inexpensive and can be purchased from most art and craft stores and even some supermarkets. See the Blue Bowl on page 63 for an illustration of its use.

I have also used flat brushes for applying a contrasting colour on the edges of some of the boxes and for blocking in the cats on the Dinner Cats place mat and coasters on page 46. I like to use sizes 6 and 8 flat brushes for this. These can be purchased from Folk Art shops where they will give you expert service and advice. My advice is to always buy the best quality brushes you can afford.

CARING FOR YOUR BRUSHES

Follow these tips to keep your brushes in tip-top condition.
- ❖ When loading, using or cleaning your brush, don't twist the hairs unnaturally.
- ❖ Do not leave your brushes sitting in water.
- ❖ Do not rest your brushes on the tips of the bristles.
- ❖ Never allow paint to dry in the brush.
- ❖ Rinse the brush in your water bucket frequently to avoid a build-up of paint near the ferrule.
- ❖ Clean your brushes promptly when you have finished painting.
- ❖ Store brushes lying flat or with their heads upright.
- ❖ Use a brush cleaner specially formulated for the medium you are using (i.e. to clean either water or oil-based mediums)

Cleaning

Hold the bristles under warm running water to remove the excess paint. Squirt a drop of brush cleaner, dishwashing liquid or liquid soap into the palm of your hand and shampoo the bristles gently, avoiding twisting and turning the bristles. Rinse and repeat. Press the ferrule of the brush gently on a scrap of white paper and if colour appears, repeat the process. When you are certain no colour remains, shape the hairs to a point with a little brush cleaner or liquid soap and leave the brush to dry with the soap still in the bristles.

PALETTE

There are many different palettes available but I like to use a wet palette. Acrylic paint has a very quick drying time, only a few minutes, which means that if you place your paints out on a dry palette you need to keep squeezing out fresh paint.

I love to use the Chezza-B Palette illustrated on the next page. This palette was designed for Folk Artists by my very dear friend Cheryl Bradshaw, and is so easy to use. Your paint will stay moist for ages—so it saves you money. All you need is a normal sponge cloth and greaseproof paper. Rinse the cloth in water, squeeze out the excess and fold a sheet of greaseproof paper around the sponge cloth, making a little parcel. Place the parcel in the recess of the palette, seam side down, and place your paints onto the greaseproof paper. When you have finished painting cover the palette until you are ready to paint next time. By opening the end of the parcel you can pour in a little more water if the sponge starts to dry out. The palette has little wells down the side so you can place any mediums you may be using in these.

Hint When basecoating I like to use cut-up milk cartons as palettes. These can be thrown away as soon as you have finished with them. Wash the carton well with warm soapy water. Cut off the top and bottom with a bread knife. Use your scissors to cut up one side and flatten out the carton. Now cut at each of the folds. You will have four great disposable palettes.

OTHER EQUIPMENT

This is a very basic list. You will probably think of other things to add to it. Most of these items are readily available from your local Art and Craft supplier. Check the list of stockists in the back of the book if you are having trouble locating an item. Most are wholesalers, but all would be able to give you the name of supplier in your area.

- sea sponge, available from chemists and supermarkets
- cotton buds for removing mistakes
- greaseproof paper, for wrapping around your sponge to make a palette and for transferring patterns
- sponge cloth
- tracing paper
- chalk pencil
- transfer paper, wax-free, e. g. Saral paper
- kneadable eraser, available from newsagents, leaves no rubbings and can be moulded
- sandpaper—1 sheet of 120 grit and one sheet of 320 grit (the higher the number the finer the paper); keep old scraps for the final sanding between layers of paint
- soft cotton rags for antiquing
- water jar
- artist's oil paint in Burnt Umber
- Scottie's Antiquing Patina
- paper towel, good quality
- wood filler (I like Timber Mate water-based wood filler)
- disposable gloves for antiquing
- 0000 steel wool
- Busy Bee Furniture Polish or Gumleaf Aromatics Natural Wood Polishing Wax
- Jo Sonja® All Purpose Sealer
- Krylon Bright White Spray Gesso
- brush cleaner—you can use dishwashing liquid or a special brush cleaner such as DecoArt™ Deco Magic

You will also need masking tape, ruler, pencil and scissors; as you progress you will add more things to your painting kit.

Equipment used in the projects in this book. Clockwise from bottom left: greaseproof paper, Chezza-B palette, Saral tracing paper, Timber Mate wood filler, French Craqueler, DecoArt Americana acrylic paints, sea sponge, spray varnish, liquid varnish, tracing paper, latex moulding, Lea Davis brush set, sponge brush, stylus, chalk pencil, kneadable eraser, oil paint

Wet palette set up: place water jar and paper towel near the hand you paint with

SURFACE PREPARATION

WOOD

I can't stress enough the need to properly prepare your surface before you begin decorating. Most of the time, beginning students are so eager to start the 'real' painting that they skip over a few of the important steps in preparing their surfaces. A properly prepared surface is a delight to paint on and will last many years, so take the time to familiarise yourself with the steps required to achieve this.

> ### SAFETY
> Always wear an apron or old shirt and a disposable mask when sanding. Sanding outdoors saves a lot of mess, but if this is not possible cover your work areas with newspaper and after sanding vacuum up the dust before going any further. Remember also—NEVER put your paintbrush in your mouth for any reason. A few colours contain cadmium or chromium which can be very dangerous if ingested over a period of time. Make it a habit not to do this and you won't have any problems.

Old wood in good condition

If you not sure whether the finish on an old wooden surface is good or bad, a simple test is to paint a small area with acrylic paint and let it dry overnight. Place a piece of sticky tape over the paint spot and pull it off. If it removes the paint then you should prepare the surface according to the directions below for wood in bad condition.

First clean off all dirt and grease. Then using medium grade sandpaper, sand lightly all over to give the new paint a firm base to adhere to. Using a sanding block saves time as well as your fingertips and enables you to sand evenly. When you come to a fiddly bit, wrap the sandpaper around your finger. Try not to sand in circles—instead, sand with the grain. If there is a dent in the wood, put a few drops of water on it and hold a steam iron a little above the surface. The water will swell the wood and the dent will disappear. Wipe off all loose sanding dust with a damp cloth. Your piece is now ready for painting.

Old wood in bad condition

If the old finish is chipped, cracked or peeling, you will have to remove it with a paint and varnish stripper. There are some great brands on the market now and you don't even have to wear gloves to use them. Ask your paint store for advice.

I would recommend always working in a well ventilated area, and reading the instruction thoroughly. Remember to remove all the hardware, that is, knobs, handle, hinges.

When you have finished stripping the piece, wash down the surface with a vinegar and water mix (about 50% water to 50% vinegar). When dry, sand well with medium grade sandpaper. Wipe over with a damp cloth to collect the sanding dust.

New wood (raw or unfinished)

Remove any labels or price tags and if they have left a sticky residue use nail polish remover to clean it off. Fill any holes with wood filler and allow to dry. If you intend to stain the wood make sure the wood filler corresponds to the stained colour. Recess any nail holes and fill these also. Sand lightly in the direction of the grain, or down the length of the piece in the case of craft wood. Be aware of any routed edges or end grain and pay special attention to them. They will need to be sanded very well. I like to use Timber Mate wood filler, and I rub this along all routed edges to help smooth them out. Sand lightly when dry.

If a super-smooth surface is required then gesso the piece after filling and sanding all the holes. Gesso seals the surface and provides great 'tooth' for the paint to adhere to. I like to use Krylon Spray Gesso in Bright White but a black gesso is also available in the Jo Sonja® range if you have to basecoat with a dark colour. Once the gesso has dried sand lightly with fine sandpaper and collect the dust with a damp cloth.

Basecoating

'To seal or not to seal—that is the question.' Most times I don't use a sealer unless the surface is rougher than usual. If this is the case I usually apply one coat of wood sealer to the surface using a sponge brush. Allow to dry, then sand well and collect the dust with a damp cloth before proceeding to paint. Some artists like to mix sealer in with their basecoat colour—you need to follow the manufacturer's instructions on the bottle to find out the recommended ratios. Adding sealer to your base colour helps reduce the sanding dust, which can be beneficial if you have health problems.

The surface is now ready for basecoating and a 50 mm (2") sponge brush is ideal for this purpose. They are inexpensive and easy to use. Squeeze out a puddle of paint onto a dry palette (remember the cut-up milk carton on page 9). Moisten the sponge brush in water and squeeze out until nearly dry. Work the paint into the brush and apply the brush to the surface using firm pressure. You may need to touch the tip of the brush in a little water to help the paint flow. If this is necessary work the water into the brush by stroking the brush back and forth on the palette before going onto your piece. Allow to dry before sanding lightly with fine sandpaper, and collect the dust with a damp cloth.

You can speed-dry the paint by blowing warm air from a hairdryer in a circular motion over the surface. Don't hold the hairdryer too close or aim it at any one spot for too long, and allow the piece to cool down before applying a second coat. Recoat following the same procedures. The instructions may ask you to apply as many coats as it takes to achieve opaque cover. This means you will need to apply as many layers of paints as necessary to make the colour uniform, not patchy. Seven or eight coats may be needed when basecoating with lighter colours.

When your budget allows you may consider purchasing a 25 mm (1") flat basecoat brush. This brush will help you achieve beautiful basecoats, but it is a little expensive.

METAL

The preparation of metal is an area which causes people a great deal of confusion. Here are some ideas to make it a little less confusing.

New metal

New metal is coated in the extrusion process with an oily protective coating which needs to be removed by washing in a solution of equal parts vinegar and water before a basecoat can be applied. Allow to dry thoroughly.

As the metal is shiny you will need to give it 'tooth' so the sealer can 'bite' onto it. Use a cream cleanser such as Jif and a scouring pad to roughen the surface slightly. There is no need to rub hard. Dry and apply one coat of Jo Sonja® All Purpose Sealer. Allow to dry. Using the Jo Sonja® tube colour of you choice, basecoat the piece until opaque cover is achieved. Set your oven to the lowest setting and place the object in the oven to cure for approximately 20 minutes. Higher temperatures may melt the solder in the seams. Allow to cool before applying the pattern. If the object is very large and won't fit in the oven, sitting it in the sun, or in the car with the windows up on a hot day, are both quite effective.

N.B. Jo Sonja® All Purpose Sealer is *not* a rust preventative. A water-based metal primer should be applied before the All Purpose Sealer if rust prevention is required. Basecoat as before.

Old metal or tin

If the tin is good condition follow the procedures for new metal. If the metal is in poor condition, rusty, or just too big a job, e.g. a trunk or a milk can, consider having it professionally treated. Some commercial establishments will sandblast and prime your items for you relatively cheaply, especially when you consider the number of hours you would need to spend yourself to make the surface suitable for painting.

If you choose to treat the piece yourself you will need to kill the rust first. An excellent rust treatment is Galmet Ironize CS, which penetrates the surface and kills the rust as well as protecting the area. First remove all flaky paint with a wire brush and apply the Ironize CS. Allow a reaction time of two or three hours. The article may be overpainted with Galmet Haloprime, which is a water-based anti-corrosive metal primer. When that is dry, basecoat in the normal way.

TRACING & TRANSFERRING A DESIGN

For tracing a design you will need:
- Greaseproof paper (*not* the waxed one, that's lunch wrap)
- Transfer paper. There are a few brands on the market but I like to use Saral. It comes in five colours but I usually use blue or white. It is available from most art and craft stores and can be used over and over. Be certain the one you are is wax-free, otherwise your paints will not adhere.
- Stylus or empty ballpoint pen
- Sharp pencil
- Ordinary blackboard chalk

TRACING THE DESIGN

The designs in this book can be traced by the following method. They can also be adapted to fit other pieces. Using greaseproof paper, trace around the perimeter of the piece you are going to decorate. Be certain to include any knobs, holes or hinges that may infringe on your design area. Fold the greaseproof paper in half lengthways and widthways, matching up with the edges of the piece. The centre of the folds is the centre of your piece. Lay the greaseproof paper over the design you have chosen in the back of the book, moving it around until the design fits into the confines of your piece and is evenly balanced. Trace the design from the book using a sharp pencil, being as accurate as possible.

TRANSFER PAPER METHOD

Secure the greaseproof paper pattern onto your piece using Blu-Tack, aligning the sides of the piece with your tracing. Slip a sheet of transfer paper, chalky side down, underneath and, using a stylus or empty ballpoint pen, trace off the design. Check to see that the design is being transferred so you can see it. Use only light pressure to avoid denting the surface and transfer only those sections of the design that are essential.

CHALK METHOD

Follow the above instructions for tracing off the design. Once the design has been traced onto greaseproof paper, turn the paper over and rub the back of it with blackboard chalk. Use a colour appropriate to the background colour of your piece. Rub in the chalk with your fingers, then shake the paper to get rid of the chalk dust. Place the greaseproof paper *chalk side down* onto your piece and using the stylus gently transfer the design.

This is a great method because you don't have to worry about tracing lines showing through your painting. The only pitfall is that the chalk is easily erased if you accidentally drop water onto it.

STROKE FORMATION

HAND AND BODY POSITION

The bench or table that you are working at should be at a height that will enable you to sit comfortably without your shoulders being hunched over. Your feet should sit flat on the floor. If your posture is incorrect you will tire quickly and won't be able to paint at your best, so take the time to make yourself comfortable.

Hold the brush perpendicular to the painting surface. Keep the weight of your hand balanced on your little finger and the side of your palm. It may feel strange at first but persevere, as this position gives excellent control. The photographs on page 21 give a good indication of the position. Don't hold the brush as you would a pencil—it should be more vertical. In the beginning you will need to keep checking on the position of the brush, but after a while it becomes second nature.

LOADING AND DRESSING THE BRUSH

1. Squeeze out a ten cent-sized puddle of paint. The consistency of the paint is very important—it should be about the consistency of thickened cream. If for some reason your brand of paint isn't like this, you will need to add enough water or medium to bring it to the correct consistency. Jo Sonja® Flow Medium, an additive that is used to thin the viscosity of paints and mediums, helps produce thinner, smoother paint.
2. Push the tip of the brush into the paint puddle and pull out a small amount of paint.
3. Work the paint into the bristles, flipping the brush from side to side, pushing the paint into the hairs, all the while stroking the brush back and forth on the palette.
4. This is called 'dressing the brush' and ensures the paint is evenly distributed throughout the hairs. Do not leaves blobs of paint clinging to the sides of the brush but rather remove them by rolling the brush towards you and tapping gently at the same time.

THINNING THE PAINT

When an instruction calls for thinned paint, you will need to add water or medium to the paint to reduce its consistency to enable long flowing strokes to be painted. Always reduce the consistency of the paint when you wish to paint long lines or thin strokes with your liner brush.

Dressing the brush correctly is very important for beautiful strokes, so spend the extra time making sure the paint is worked through the hairs.

STROKE FORMATION WITH THE ROUND BRUSH

Comma stroke

With the brush correctly dressed and held in the correct vertical position, press the tip of the brush down onto your practice paper and pause a moment to let the hairs fan out. Gradually pull the brush towards you, releasing pressure and lifting simultaneously. Slow down near the middle of the stroke to allow the hairs to come back into alignment and so avoid scraggy tails. Your comma stroke should look like mine in the illustration on the next page, but if it doesn't, check what went wrong and try again. Remember—persevere and practise!

What went wrong:
1. Body of the comma is too long. Lift the brush up after the head of the comma is formed.
2. Brush was laid down to the ferrule—too far. Stay up on the tip of the brush, using pressure to fan out the hairs, rather than laying the brush down.
3. Stroke is too curved—point the tail of the comma towards the bottom of the paper.
4. This is a 'walking stick' stroke. The brush was laid down to the ferrule and then the tail flipped under. Slow down and use pressure on the hairs rather than laying the brush down.

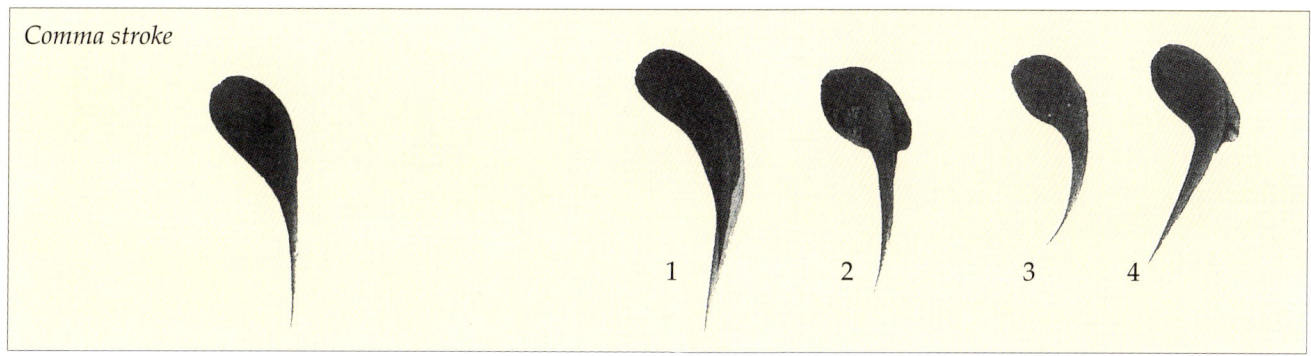

Daisy stroke

The brush must leave the palette with the hairs rounded. Press down on the paper to fan out the hairs, as for the comma stroke; now, release the pressure and pull the brush towards you, at the same time rolling your thumb forward and twisting the brush half a turn. The brush should roll between your finger and thumb. Don't tuck your thumb behind your index finger.

What went wrong:
1 Pressure was released too quickly. It should change gradually.
2 The thumb was tucked behind the index finger so that when forced, it jumped and control was lost.
3 This stroke was pulled before the hairs had a chance to fan out—remember to pause.

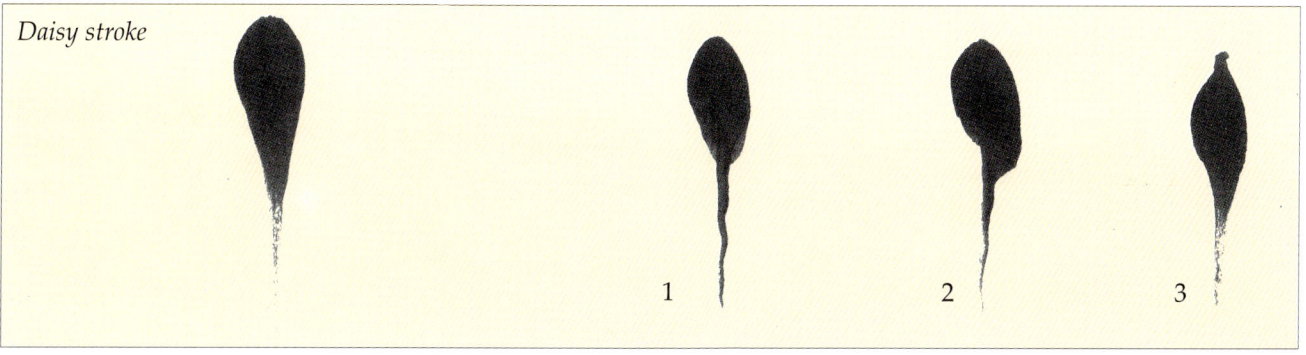

S-stroke

The brush must leave the palette with the hairs flattened. Stroke the bristles over the palette until they flatten out. You are really making a flat brush with a chisel edge. Starting on the chisel, move to the right in this case (but you can go either way), applying pressure as you move down. Slow down and level off, keeping on the chisel.

What went wrong:
1 The brush left the palette rounded, not flattened.
2 Slow down at the bottom and allow the hairs to flatten out.

BRUSH STROKE WORKSHEET

To get the best out of this round brush worksheet photocopy it so you won't get paint on your book. Place the photocopy inside a plastic sleeve and lay a square of greaseproof paper over it, taping it securely on either side, so you can see the strokes clearly through the paper. I suggest you photocopy the worksheet at different sizes so you can practise larger and smaller strokes with different brushes.

Check the 'What went wrong' sections if your strokes don't look right. Here is a checklist.

1. *Make sure the brush is dressed correctly. See page 14.*
2. *Check the position of the brush. You should be holding it upright, not on the same angle as a pen.*
3. *Rest lightly on you little finger and the outside of your palm.*
4. *Follow the direction listed for each stroke.*

C-stroke

The brush leaves the palette with the hairs flattened (a chisel edge). Move to the left, apply pressure, slow down, and chisel to the right. It may be easier for left-handed painters to reverse these instructions.

What went wrong:
1 Too much pressure at the beginning of the stroke.
2 Concentrate on making both ends the same.

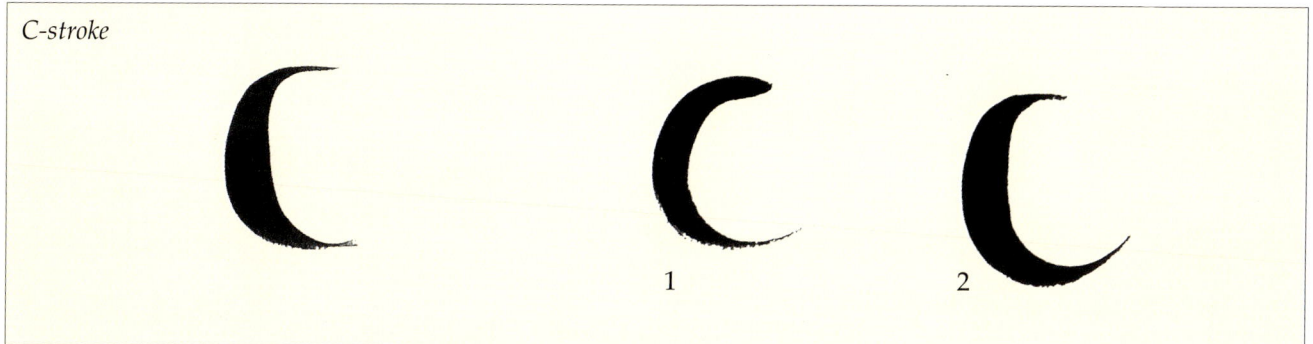

C-stroke

STROKE FORMATION WITH THE LINER BRUSH

Comma stroke

This comma stroke was painted with paint straight from the puddle—the paint was worked into the hairs.

What went wrong:
1 Too much water for a comma stroke, but perfect for cross-hatching or liner work. No bulk in the stroke.
2 Hairs were laid down to ferrule. Keep up on tip.

Teardrops (sit-downs)

Leave the palette with a point on the brush, and keep up on the tip (it helps if there is plenty of paint in the middle section of the brush). Slow down and apply pressure, then lift and straighten up.

What went wrong:
1 Hairs pushed back up when lifting off. Slow down.
2 Remember: come to a complete stop before lifting off.

S-stroke

The principle is the same as for the S-stroke with the round brush, but start off on the tip and apply increased pressure for increased thickness. Slow down and lift off to finish. Top and bottom of stroke should look the same.

What went wrong:
1 Maintain even pressure so that top and bottom match.
2 The brush left the palette rounded, so the beginning is too heavy. Stay up on the tip.

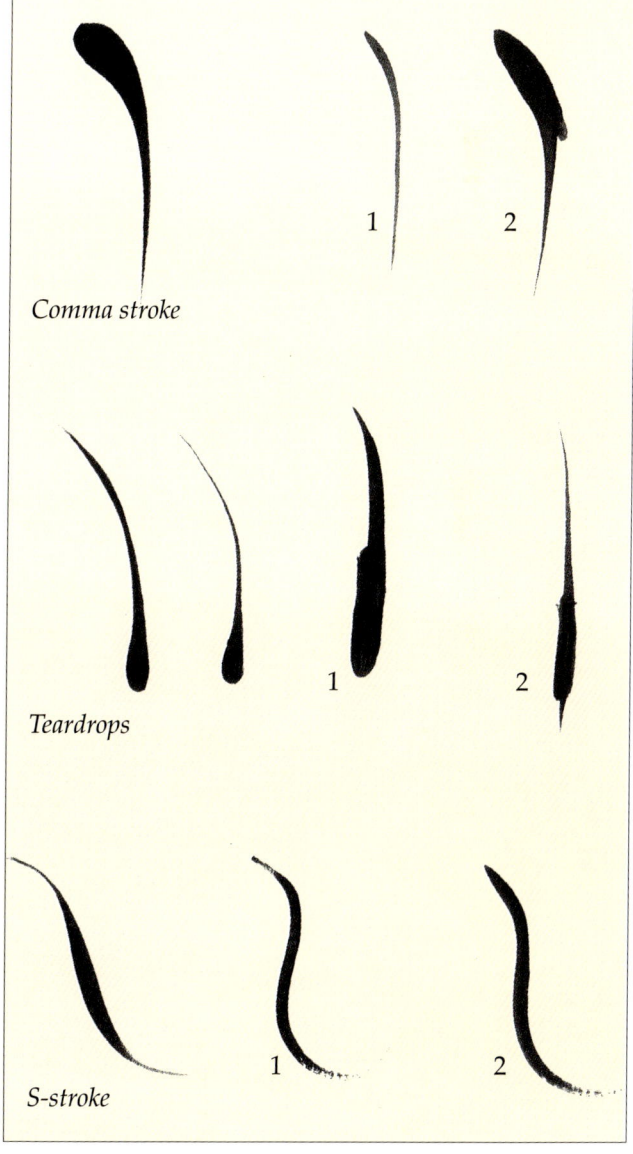

Swirls and tendrils

Swirls and tendrils
Use thinned paint and keep your hand and arm off the table. You will need to think about the following hint, but it works—lock your elbow and wrist and move from the shoulder.

What went wrong:
1 Uneven pressure from poor hand and arm position.

Horizontal stroke
Leave the palette with a point on the brush. Keep on the tip, then apply pressure until the middle of the stroke, slowly decreasing from the middle to the end. Remember, by applying pressure you increase the width of the stroke.

What went wrong:
1 Too fast at the end. Slow down.

Cross-hatching
The paint must be thinned with water or medium for successful cross-hatching. Fill the brush up to the ferrule. Stay up on the tip and keep the brush vertical.

What went wrong:
1 Paint is too thick.
2 Uneven pressure and paint too thick.

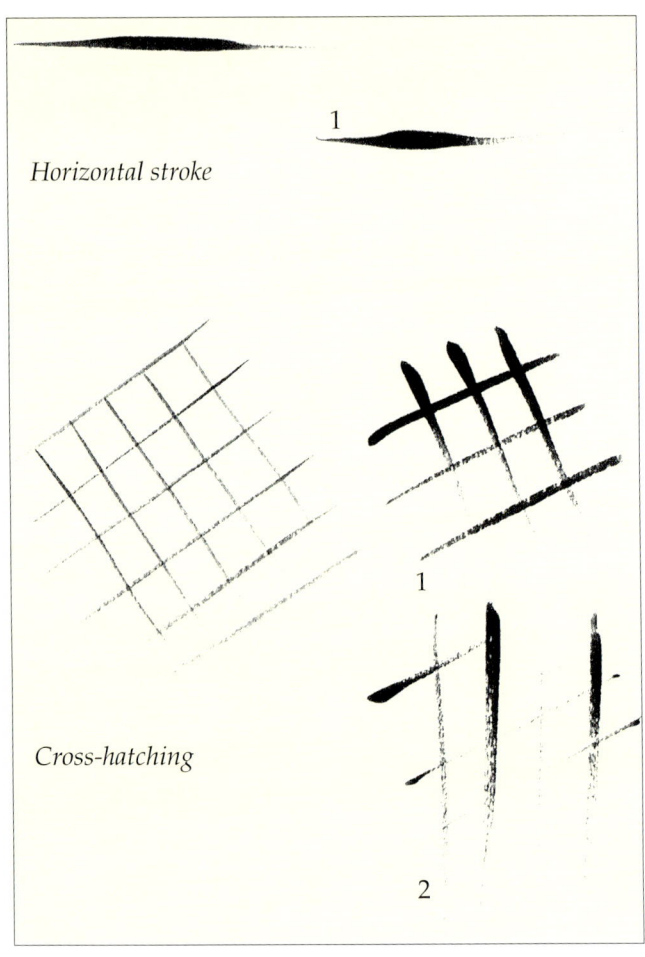

Horizontal stroke

Cross-hatching

SPECIAL BRUSH TECHNIQUES

Sideloading (round brush)

Now you have practised the beginning strokes you should feel comfortable with your brush and know what it can and can't do. Sideloading is a little tricky in the beginning but is well worth persevering with. Here we go.

Place out a puddle of a dark colour, say Williamsburg Blue, and a light colour such as Titanium White. Dress the no. 5 round brush with Williamsburg Blue. This will give good contrast to the white sideload. To sideload, push the brush horizontally into the puddle of Titanium White paint and pull it out towards your shoulder, lifting it off the palette rather than dragging it. It helps to have a strip of paint rather than a puddle. You should have white on only one side of the brush, as in the diagram. If you drag the brush through the puddle or strip of paint you will wipe off some of the darker colour and blend the colours together a little. Look at the brush to make certain that the white is only on one side of the brush. If it isn't, wash out the brush and start again.

Now holding the white to the top of the page, not to the ceiling (see diagram 2), practise pulling comma strokes. The strokes should have the white down the right or left side, depending on which way you pulled the comma. See diagram 3.

Both paints must be of the same consistency or one will slide off the other. If this occurs put out fresh paint.

If you roll the brush after sideloading, you will get a similar effect to tipping the brush with paint (see page 22). Aim for a nice ridge down one side of the stroke.

What went wrong:
1. Brush was rolled under so blending occurred and the white was lost halfway down the stroke.
2. The white was held to the ceiling, not to the top of the page.
3. The white was held towards the bottom of the page, not to the top.

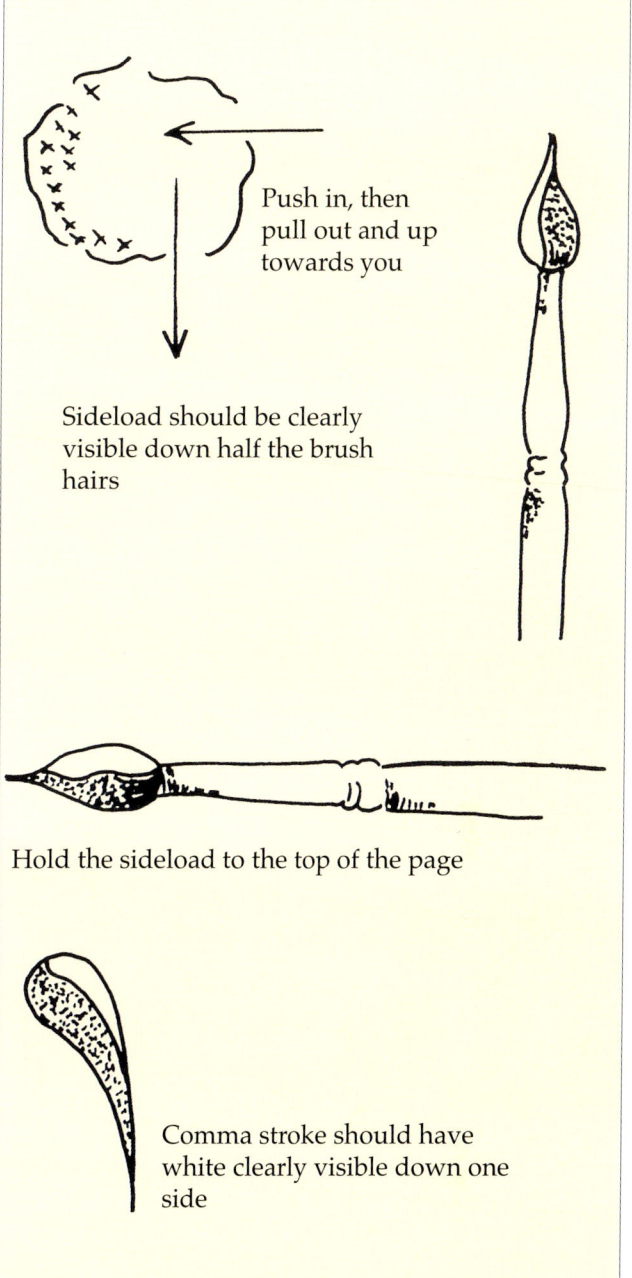

Sideload should be clearly visible down half the brush hairs

Hold the sideload to the top of the page

Comma stroke should have white clearly visible down one side

Side loading with the round brush

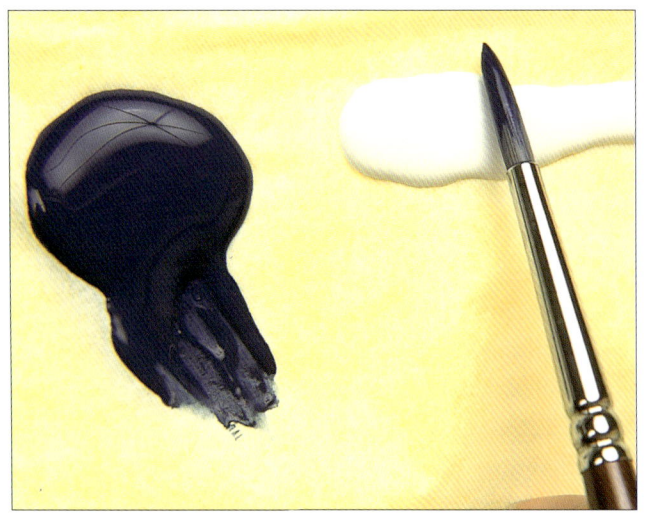

1. Place paint out in a strip

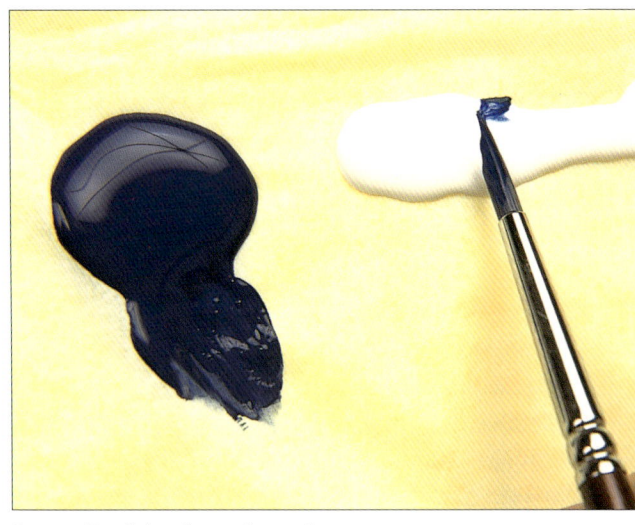

2. Push in along the strip

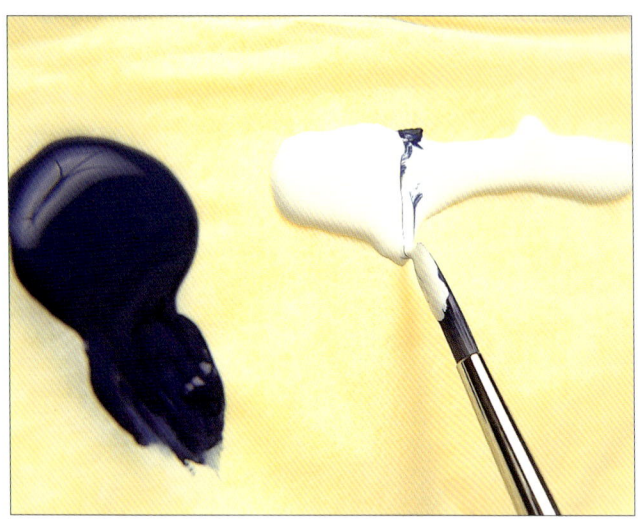

3. Lift out

4. Starting the stroke

5. Halfway through the stroke

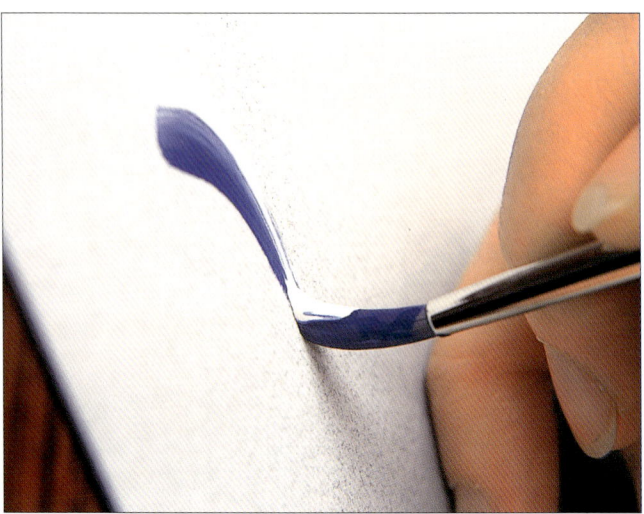

6. Finishing the stroke—notice the white is held to the outside of the stroke

Pull-in

The pull-in style (usually used for flower petals) is harder again than sideloading but is my favourite style. There are a few things to remember:

1. Aim for a thick ridge of paint around the edge of the petals. As you perfect this technique you will decrease the amount of paint needed to get the same effect.
2. Wipe off all excess paint on paper towelling. Try to keep out of the water jar unless you find the brush dragging across your work when pulling down the colour. To rectify this, touch the tip of the brush in a tiny bead of water (I shake a few drops onto my palette before I start painting) and work it into the hairs by stroking the hairs back and forth on the palette.
3. Spread the hairs on the brush by stroking the brush back and forth in the flower colour—this is called sweeping. The hairs will flatten and splay out.
4. Push out the ridge of paint around *one* petal at a time. Don't try and edge any more than this in the beginning, or the ridge will dry before you have time to pull it down.

Squeeze out two colours onto your palette—we'll use Williamsburg Blue and Titanium White again. Using the no. 5 brush, dress the brush in Williamsburg Blue and sideload in Titanium White. Hold the brush so that the sideload of white is facing towards the outside of the petal. Apply pressure to the brush to push the white off as you move around the pattern line (first photograph). Wipe off the excess white paint on paper towel and sweep (see point 3 above) through Williamsburg Blue two or three times. The hairs should be flattened or fanned out. Push these fanned-out hairs under the thick ridge of white paint and pull the colour down to the middle of the flower (second photograph). Wipe off excess paint, sweep through Williamsburg Blue and repeat.

You don't have to reload each time, rather keep an eye out for when the petal is beginning to look too light; when this happens, wipe off the excess paint on paper towel, sweep through the flower colour again and keep on going.

Make sure the strokes come down to the middle of the flower and follow the shape of the petal, as in the second photo. With this technique you must be certain to paint the petals at the back or underneath first, so the ones in front will cover the raggy ends. I have included numbers on many of the patterns to show the petal painting sequence.

Pull-in, step 1—Pushing off a thick ridge of paint

Pull-in, step 2—Splay brush, tuck it under the thick ridge of paint and pull the white down

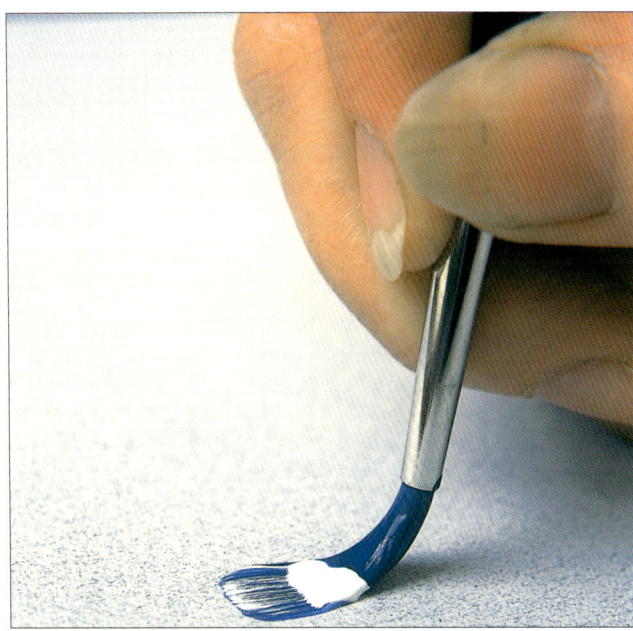

Tipping the brush—Notice white held towards the ceiling

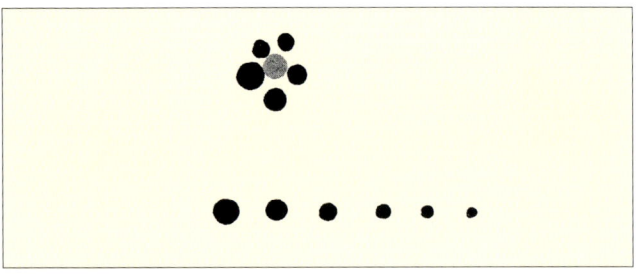

Tipping

The tipping technique is the same for round and liner brushes. Load the brush in the main colour, e.g. for a leaf use green, then wipe the tip of the brush in a second colour, say white.

Paint the stroke. You will have green streaked with white. Using the two leaf colours from the example, if you hold the white to look to the ceiling you will have more white in the stroke; conversely, if you hold the white to look to the surface you will have more green in the stroke.

Tip the brush in clean white each time you reload, or you will be making pale green on your palette by going over and over into the same area of white.

Dots

Use fresh paint and the handle of your paintbrush if it comes to a point. Consider also a stylus or empty ball-point pen.

Dip it into the middle of the puddle and set down onto the paper. The dot will decrease in size each time you put the handle to the paper. Five dots in a circle with a contrasting dot in the middle make a very simple flower.

Sweeping

This technique is one I use all the time because I am basically a very lazy painter and don't like to pick up and put down different brushes. If you practise this technique later on you can do all your painting with only one brush. In the following description I will use the colours Williamsburg Blue, Yellow Light and Titanium White, in that order.

Load the size 3 brush in the main colour—which is Williamsburg Blue because it is listed first. Look at the brush and you will see that the bristles are rounded. With the tip of the brush pull out a little Yellow Light from the puddle and place it down on a clean area on the palette. Sweep or wipe the hairs over this using the same side of the brush to push the paint in—don't twist or turn the brush. Don't try and load the paint in the brush—just wipe the brush in the Yellow Light. Look at the brush again and you will see that it has flattened out and now has two sides—a red side and a yellowish side. Sideload in a little Titanium White using the yellowish side of the brush and with the white facing towards the surface, sweep the white into the hairs as you did with the yellow. The brush hairs should still be flattened so you still have two sides. Do not aim for a great deal of paint coverage when sweeping. By turning the brush a quarter of a turn and holding it upright you will be able to paint very fine lines such as the veins on the leaves. Sometimes you need only sweep through one colour but if more colours are mentioned in the instructions it is important to sweep through them in the order stated.

BACKGROUND TECHNIQUES

There are several very easy yet interesting techniques that decorative painters use to enhance the background surface of their pieces.

SPONGING

Sponging is a very simple and effective faux finish that is done using a natural sea sponge. Sea sponges are preferable to synthetic sponges because their holes are uneven in size and the texture can vary greatly from one area of the sponge to another, while synthetic sponges are uniform and give a regular, uninteresting pattern. Sponging can be done using one, two or three colours depending on the look you wish to create. A lovely soft background effect is achieved by moistening the surface of your piece with a little water first and then sponging on another colour.

You will need:
- natural sea sponge
- acrylic paints
- dry palette made from a milk carton (see page 9)
- sponge brush for basecoating
- mop brush (optional)

Method
1. Sand the surface of your piece and collect the dust with a damp cloth.
2. Use the sponge brush and your chosen colour to basecoat your piece.
3. Wet the sea sponge and wring out the excess water. Pour out a little of your first sponging colour onto a dry palette. Pounce the sponge up and down in this, then move onto a clean area of the palette and pounce the sponge up and down again to evenly distribute the paint throughout the sponge.
4. Now sponge over your piece, moving your hand around to avoid a repeat pattern. Reload as often as necessary, making certain to pounce the sponge on a clean area of the palette to distribute the paint evenly within it.
5. If you have chosen to sponge with more than one colour, pour a little of the second colour out onto the palette. Don't wash the sponge, but rather pounce it into this second colour and continue on as before, remembering to work the colour into the sponge as in step 3.
6. For each succeeding colour repeat above instructions.
7. For a softer finish mop the wet paint with a mop brush to gently blur the sponging.

FAUX FINISH WITH PLASTIC WRAP

This is an easy faux finish that adds an interesting effect to your work. I sometimes like to finish the inside or underneath of my pieces using this technique as it looks great and is quick to complete.

You will need:
- plastic kitchen wrap
- DecoArt™ Faux Glazing Medium or Jo Sonja® Clear Glazing Medium (optional)
- dry palette (see page 9)
- sponge brush

Method
1. Sand piece well and collect the dust with a damp cloth.
2. Basecoat your piece in your chosen colour. I have used DecoArt™ Americana Williamsburg Blue in the example.
3. Mix enough water into the second colour paint to reduce the consistency. I have used DecoArt™ Americana Sand. You will need to play with this ratio a little—too much paint will give an almost solid cover whereas too much water will dilute the paint so much you won't see anything once the surface has dried. You can also mix DecoArt™ Faux Glazing Medium into the paint, which will give a different effect. The Faux Glazing Medium holds the pattern left by the plastic wrap so the effect is more obvious. I suggest you try both methods to see which one you like best.

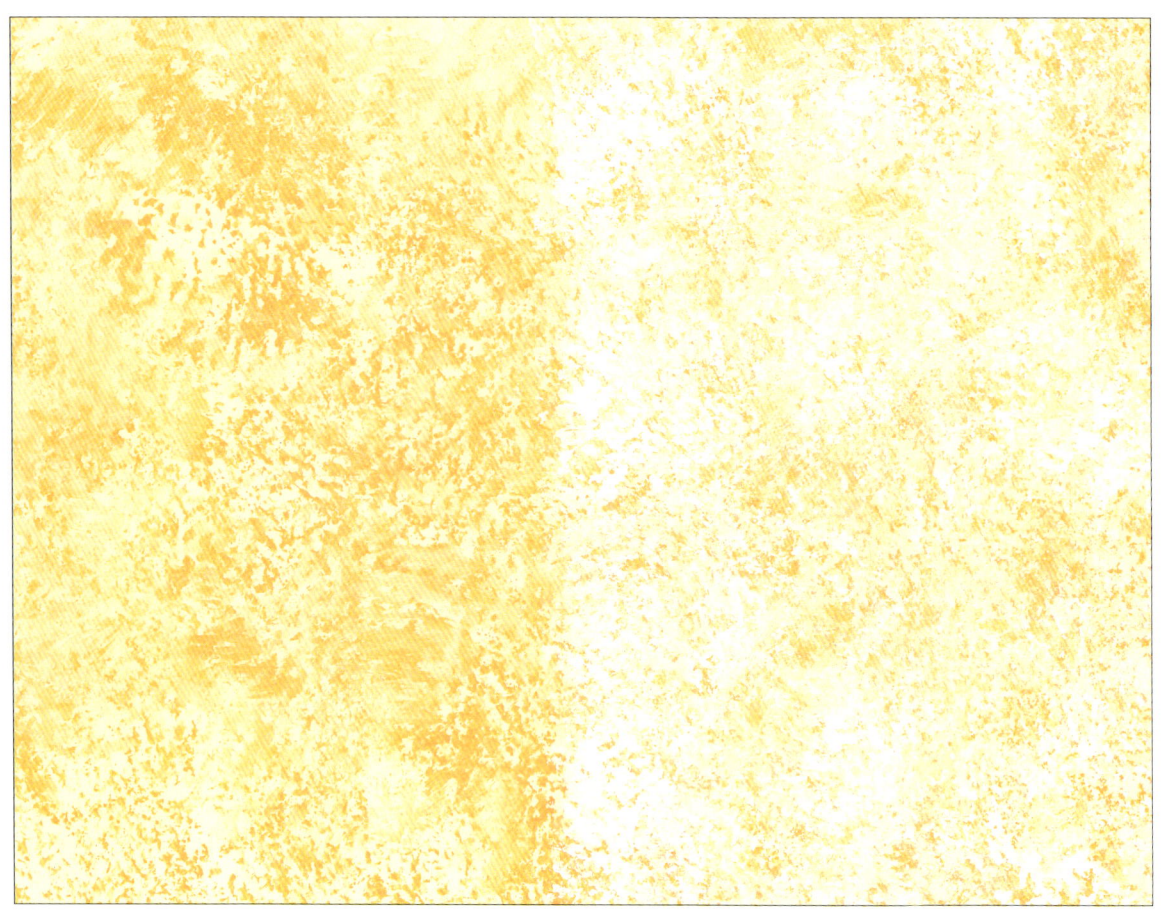

Sponging (basecoat Sand, first sponging Antique Gold, second sponging Titanium White)

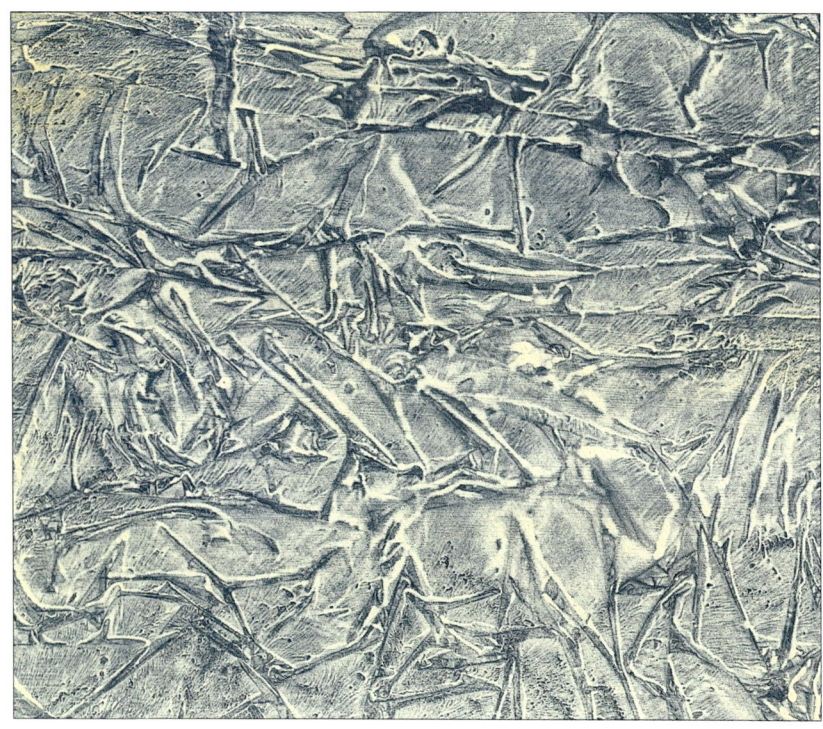

Faux finish with plastic wrap (basecoat Williamsburg Blue, top coat Sand)

4. Using the sponge brush apply the paint mix to the surface of your piece, working one surface at a time.
5. Working quickly before it has time to dry, tear off a big enough section of plastic wrap to cover the wet surface, and gently press it onto the surface.
6. Lift off the plastic wrap and discard. You should now have a great faux finish that looks a little like marble. If you don't like what you have done and the paint is still wet, simply brush on another coat and repeat the process. Dry with the hairdryer and finish each surface of your piece as before.
7. When you are satisfied with the appearance of the finish, dry all surfaces thoroughly with the hairdryer. If the faux finish plastic wrap surface is to be painted over decoratively, I suggest painting a barrier coat of DecoArt™ Faux Glazing Medium over the dried faux finish. This will enable you to remove any mistakes that may occur when you are painting your design without disturbing the plastic wrap effect underneath.

CRISS-CROSS BACKGROUND

This is one of my favourite background techniques. You can use almost any combination of colours depending on the effect you wish to achieve. I painted the Blue Bowl on page 63 using this technique—I hope you like it.

You will need:
- dry palette (see page 9)
- colours of your choice. I have used DecoArt™ Williamsburg Blue, Titanium White and Sand on this example.
- 25 mm (1") cheap bristle brush (available from the supermarket or art and craft stores).

Method
1. On a dry palette squeeze out a little of all three colours.
2. Load the bristle brush with a little of all three colours—it doesn't matter in which order you load them or on what side of the brush.
3. Paint the surface of your piece in a series of Xs, picking up more colour as you need it. If the area you are working in is getting too blue, then pick up a little more Sand or Titanium White, and vice versa. Aim for a soft mottled effect with a little of each colours visible throughout.
4. You may need to skim over the surface from time to time to smooth out any textured areas. You could also use a mop brush to do this.
5. Dry and repeat if you feel it is necessary.

Criss-cross background technique, using DecoArt™ Americana colours—Williamsburg Blue, Titanium White and Sand

ANTIQUING

Antiquing gives your finished piece an aged appearance, imparting the same depth of tone to all the colours. There are two ways of doing this, using oil-based or water-based products.

OIL ANTIQUING

This method uses oil-based products and should be completed in a well ventilated area. Wear disposable gloves. When the antiquing is finished, throw the gloves and all the rags and papers you have used in the outside rubbish bin. Wet them thoroughly with water first, as cases of spontaneous combustion have been reported from time to time.

Even though this method usually removes graphite lines, it is a good idea to remove them first with a kneadable eraser.

You will need
- Scotties Antiquing Patina Medium, Boyle Antiquing Patina or Chroma's Odourless Patina for Folk and Decorative Artists
- oil paints by either Winsor and Newton or Rowney. I like to use Burnt Umber, but consider also Raw Umber (which has a greenish cast to it), Burnt Sienna (which is much redder) or Prussian Blue (looks great on pieces basecoated in blue).
- dry palette (see page 9)
- squares of lint-free cotton cloth, and plenty of them
- bristle brush, approximately 12 mm (½")
- DecoArt™ Faux Glazing Medium or Jo Sonja® Clear Glazing Medium

A few hints before you start:
- Have everything prepared before you start. I sometimes save a few pieces and antique them all at the one time.
- Work one surface at a time. Oil paints take much longer to dry than acrylics and it's very easy to leave finger marks on a surface which has been newly antiqued.
- If you feel the result is too dark you can remove most of the oil antiquing by moistening a clean cloth with Antiquing Patina (or Patina Medium, whichever one you are using) and wiping it over the surface. Don't leave it to dry before you decide you don't like it—the oil paint must be removed fairly quickly.
- You can apply a barrier coat of DecoArt™ Faux Glazing Medium or Jo Sonja® Clear Glazing Medium to protect the decorative painting underneath before you start antiquing. Once your painting is all finished, allow to dry. Apply one even coat of Faux Glazing or Clear Glazing Medium to all surfaces using the sponge brush or a large flat brush. There is a slight risk sometimes, especially if you have thinned your acrylic paint with water, that the Antiquing Patina may remove some of the lines. Covering the surface with a barrier coat prevents this.

Method
These instructions apply to all three products.
1. Moisten a small square of clean cotton cloth with Patina Medium. Wipe this over the area to be antiqued, making sure the entire surface has been covered, and leaving no puddles or drips. For the corners of boxes and any routed edges, you will need to dip a bristle brush in the Patina Medium and use it to get into all the corners and grooves.
2. Squeeze out a small blob of Burnt Umber oil paint onto a dry palette and using the area on the cotton cloth that has the Patina Medium on it, pick up a small amount of the oil paint. Rub the cloth and oil paint on a clean area of the dry palette to work the paint into the cloth.
3. Wipe over the surface of your piece with the paint-smeared cloth. Most of your painting will disappear beneath a brown cover of paint, but don't be alarmed. Most people seeing antiquing demonstrated for the first time throw up their arms in horror, thinking that their masterpiece has been ruined. Not so! Use the bristle brush tapped into a little oil paint to reach into the corners and crevices.

4. Take a clean cotton cloth and smooth out the antiquing to the desired depth of colour. Rub a little harder in the centre of the design to remove more of the antiquing there, leaving the outside edges darker. If you would like certain areas lighter, remove the antiquing with a cotton bud dipped in the Patina Medium.
5. Leave oil antiquing to dry for at least four or five days—longer in cold weather. When dry, varnish with an oil-compatible varnish such as DecoArt™ DuraClear.

WATER-BASED ANTIQUING

This method of antiquing dries much more quickly than oil antiquing, but doesn't give the same rich mellow effect (perhaps I'm a little biased). Because the mediums used are water-based products there is no problem with smell. I would advise you to try both methods and see for yourself which one you prefer.

You will need:
- Jo Sonja® Retarder and Antiquing Medium
- Jo Sonja® Tube Paint in the colour of your choice—consider Brown Earth, Burnt Umber, Burnt Sienna or Raw Sienna
- Jo Sonja® Clear Glazing Medium
- dry palette (see page 9)
- clean rags
- sponge brush
- large mop brush (optional)—this is a large soft brush, much like a make-up brush, which is used to soften any streaks that may occur
- Jo Sonja® Polyurethane Water-Based Satin Varnish (optional)

Method
1. Allow the finished painted article to dry overnight or longer. Using the sponge brush apply one even coat of Clear Glazing Medium and allow to dry thoroughly. Clear Glazing Medium acts as a barrier coat, protecting your precious artwork underneath. Mix your chosen Jo Sonja® tube acrylic paint with Retarder and Antiquing Medium to the desired depth of colour. Try mixing 1 part Retarder and Antiquing Medium to 1 part Brown Earth. Test a small area of your work (say, inside or underneath) to see if the colour's transparency is correct. If it isn't dark enough for your liking add more paint; if too dark, add more Retarder.
2. Using the sponge brush apply the antiquing mix evenly over the surface, working one surface at a time.
3. Start to wipe back immediately, using a clean lint-free cloth. Any areas that need to be highlighted can be wiped out with a water-moistened cotton bud and the edges softened with the mop brush.
4. Just as Retarder and Antiquing Medium slows the drying time of the paints and mediums used with it, so also it affects any product used over it. To minimise the risk of problems occurring, allow 7 to 10 days for the surface to dry out before applying Jo Sonja® Polyurethane Water-Based Satin Varnish with either the sponge brush or a large flat brush.

SELECTIVE ANTIQUING

I have used this technique on the Dinner Cats project on page 46. It can be used to shade around an area to create depth and is a very quick and easy way to achieve an effect.

You will need
- supplies as listed for oil antiquing above
- cotton buds
- small flat brush, size 2 or 4
- mop brush

Method
1. Antique the piece as in the instructions above.
2. Decide where you would like to create a shadow. This is usually on the underneath section of an area, e.g. where one petal overlaps the other, you would shade along the overlap on the underneath petal. The petal that sits on top will now be lighter and appear to come forward. In the case of the Dinner Cats I have used shading under the chins and along the legs.
3. Use the small flat brush and work a small amount of oil paint into the hairs. Paint this in your chosen shade are, keeping the paint confined to that particular area only. Clean up any paint that inadvertently strays onto the highlight area with a cotton bud.
4. Soften the painted line with a cotton bud, gently pulling the paint out from the line a little way to create a gradation of colour.
5. Use the mop brush to gently whisk away any lines, remembering to use very light pressure—as if you were dusting the brush over the surface. You should now have a shaded area that is dark in the darkest shadow area, fading away to nothing as you move away from the shadow area.

GILDING

The method I have used on the faux finish coasters on page 44 is very easy and great fun to do. If your require more information on gilding I suggest you either borrow a book from your local library or purchase a book from your local bookstore. *The Glory of Gold* by Sue Trytell (Sally Milner Publishing, 1995) is a great 'how-to' book if you would like to learn more.

You will need
- metal leaf—I like to use Dutch metal (imitation gold), but consider also copper leaf, aluminium leaf and

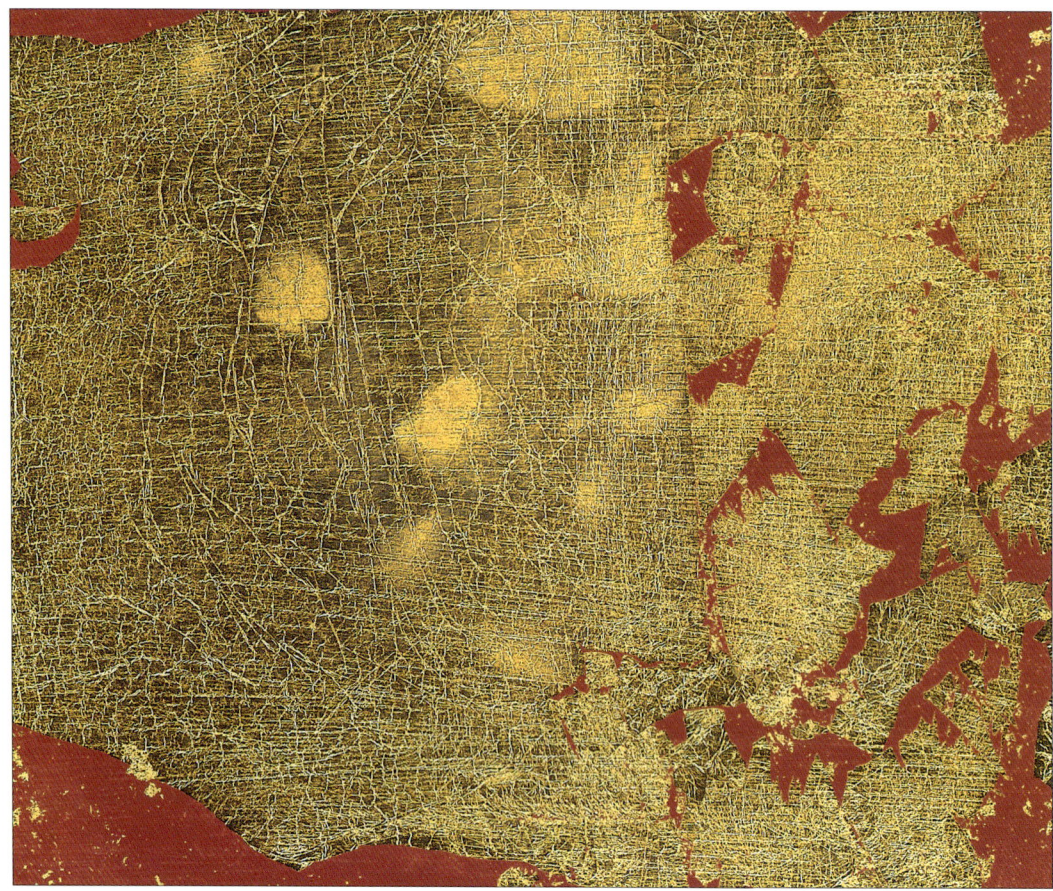

Solid cover　　　　　　　　　　Broken cover
Gilding (basecoat DecoArt™ Red Iron Oxide)

variegated leaf—these can be purchased either as single sheets or in books of 25 sheets
- white cotton gloves, available quite cheaply from chemists and sometimes from supermarkets
- Jo Sonja® Tannin Blocking Sealer for Wood
- flat brush for applying the Tannin Blocking Sealer; the size of the brush will be determined by the size of the article you wish to gild.
- base paint in the colour of your choice; it is important to choose a colour that will harmonise with your decorative painting because the colour will show through the cracks in the gold leaf. The base colour may also influence the final 'glow' of the gold. I have used DecoArt™ Red Iron Oxide in my example
- large mop brush for dusting off the excess gold leaf.
- large flat brush or a sponge brush for basecoating your piece.

Method
1. Sand the surface well and collect the sanding dust with a damp cloth.
2. Using the sponge or large flat basecoating brush, basecoat the surface of your piece with at least two coats, sanding well in between. The colour in the example is Red Iron Oxide.
3. Using the appropriate size flat brush for the piece you are about to gild, coat the surface with one even coat of Jo Sonja® Tannin Blocking Sealer. Allow to dry.
4. Apply one more smooth even coat and again allow to touch dry.
5. Put on the cotton gloves and, holding the gold leaf by the paper backing, slide a sheet of leaf onto the surface of your piece. Repeat this procedure until the entire surface or area which you wish to gild has been covered.
6. Using the mop brush lightly dust over the surface, pushing the gold leaf down into any crevices or routed edges with a gentle tapping motion.
7. Sweep all the skewings (leftover bits of gold leaf) together and save them to decorate smaller items such as pencils or brooches. If there any large areas where the gold leaf hasn't stuck simply apply more Tannin Blocking Sealer, allow to touch dry and press on a piece of gold leaf.
8. Varnish as normal with your usual varnish.

FINISHING TECHNIQUES

VARNISHING

There are many types of varnish available but the idea behind them all is to protect your finished piece with a tough coating. There are four types of finish to choose from:
❖ matte—dull with no shine
❖ satin—a soft glow resembling a hand-rubbed finish (my favourite)
❖ semi-gloss—a slight shine, and
❖ gloss—a bright shine

Not all varnishes are available in all four finishes.

Water-based varnishes are the easiest to use and DecoArt™ Duro Clear is perfect for most of my needs. It is an exterior/interior clear polyurethane varnish that dries quickly and is suitable for use over oil antiquing.

Spray varnishes are also very popular and give a lovely finish. If you decide to use a spray varnish please adhere to the safety directions faithfully and spray outdoors. Spray varnishes dry very quickly so multiple coats can be applied in a short space of time. Remember to spray lightly, as spraying too heavily causes runs.

Before you start to varnish a piece, make certain that it is thoroughly dry, and check that there are no transfer lines visible. I have been nearly ready to varnish on quite a few occasions and at the last minute have noticed a few stray lines that I had not erased properly.

I usually apply water-based varnish with a sponge brush. If you are using an oil-based varnish you will have to use a 25 mm (1") flat brush as sponge brushes can disintegrate with disastrous results. Whichever you choose, the article must be completely dry before you start. Remember also to varnish in a warm room as 'blooming' can occur if the surrounding air is too cold. Blooming, cloudy streaks through the varnish, is caused by moisture trapped in the varnish because the air was too cold or there was too much humidity in the air.

Work in a well lit room so you can see any streaks or fluff that may land on your piece. Use light coats rather than thick ones, waiting for the recommended length of time before applying the next one. Most pieces will need at least three coats, but for an alcohol-resistant surface five or six coats are preferable.

I like to wax some of my varnished pieces—this surface feels wonderful. To do this you need a good quality paste wax and 0000 steel wool. Allow the varnish to dry at least overnight, longer in cold weather, then take a small piece of steel wool, rub in the paste wax, then rub all over the surface of your piece. Allow the wax to dry for at least an hour or more then buff to a soft shine with a piece of old cotton cloth.

STAINING

Light coloured woods may be stained before painting decoratively. There are quite a few methods one may choose so I will give only a few examples here.

Jo Sonja® Clear Glazing Medium and Retarder

Combine 3 parts Jo Sonja® Clear Glazing Medium with 1 part Retarder and Antiquing Medium and 1 part colour of your choice and mix together thoroughly. Use a sponge brush to apply this mix to the surface and wipe off with a clean cloth, making sure to wipe with the grain. The Retarder and Antiquing Medium added to the mixture keeps the stain mix workable longer.

If you find the effect is too dark, moisten a clean cloth with water and rub over the surface of the wood. This process won't take off all the colour but will lighten it considerably if you haven't left it too long. Always remember the end grain of the wood will stain much darker than the flat surface.

You can stain with any colour or combinations of colours—be adventurous. If you are wanting to simulate natural wood colours then try combinations of the earth colours—Jo Sonja® Raw Umber plus Brown Earth mixed together gives a lovely walnut colour, for example. Consider any of the earth colours—Raw Sienna, Burnt Umber, Red Earth.

If you want only a very light stain, seal the surface with one coat of Clear Glazing Medium before applying the stain. Because the more porous end grain will stain darker, seal this with a coat of Clear Glazing Medium as well.

Pre-mixed stains

Pre-mixed stains are nice to use and there is a wide variety to choose from. DecoArt™ Gel Stain comes in six colours as well as a clear base, so you can mix your own if you prefer. You can also antique with Gel Stains.

Pour out a puddle of Gel Stain onto a dry palette. Use a sponge brush to apply the stain to the wood surface, then wipe off with a clean cloth in the direction of the grain.

CRACKLING
illustrated on page 31

Crackling is another area that causes confusion. Basically there are three types of crackle products available. Each one performs differently and you need to know the effect you want to achieve and match it to the appropriate product. All the paint manufacturers recommend using *only* their acrylic paints in conjunction with their crackle mediums. As with any medium you are not familiar with, please experiment a little before using on a project piece. Please refer to the examples in the illustrations.

Sandwich crackle

The sample has been painted using DecoArt™ Americana Acrylics and DecoArt™ Weathered Wood as the crackle product. This type of crackle is called a sandwich crackle because the medium, in this case Weathered Wood, sits between two layers of paint. The crackle effect is more obvious if a light colour is painted over a dark colour or vice versa.

Method
1. Paint the surface with your chosen colour. I have used Sand. Allow to dry and recoat if necessary. Sand lightly and collect the dust with a damp cloth. Dry.
2. Using the sponge brush apply one even coat of Weathered Wood. Allow this to dry for at least 20 minutes, and up to 60 minutes, depending on the temperature.
3. Using either a large flat brush or sponge brush, apply a contrasting top coat. I have used Antique Gold in the example. If you apply the paint up and down, the cracks will travel in that direction; conversely, if the paint is applied from left to right, the cracks will run that way. You may touch up any missed areas immediately but be careful not to overbrush.
4. Another method of applying the top coat is to sponge your chosen colour over the Weathered Wood. This will produce finer random cracks. Moisten a sea sponge with water and wring out until quite dry. Pounce the sponge in your chosen colour, tap on a clean area of the palette to work the colour into the sponge, then sponge the colour over the Weathered Wood again, being careful not to overwork any area.

Top coat crackle

This product is used to simulate the effects of aging and produces fine or crazed patterns when applied over decorative painting or a painted surface. I have used Jo Sonja® Crackle Medium and Jo Sonja® Yellow Oxide acrylic paint in the example.
1. Sand the surface thoroughly and collect the sanding dust with a damp cloth.
2. Apply three or four heavy coats of basecoat paint quickly, applying the next layer as soon as the previous one has dried to the touch. It is important *not* to speed-dry the layers with a heater or hairdryer as this will cure the paint too fast for the Crackle Medium to work.
3. Decorate with the required pattern and allow your painting to dry—but don't let the paint dry overnight before attempting to crackle.
4. Apply a heavy coat of Crackle Medium over the surface or area to be crackled, using a large soft brush. The medium goes on milky but dries clear. This product works best when allowed to dry naturally but you can use a hairdryer if you wish.
5. When the crackle surface is dry, sand the surface gently using #400 or #600 grit wet and dry sandpaper and blow away the sanding dust.
6. You may antique the surface for that final touch, but it's not essential.

Note Surfaces such as knotty pine, chipboard and Masonite need to be sealed with Jo Sonja® Tannin Blocking Sealer before you begin the crackling or painting process. Crackle Medium will pull the pitch (resin) from these surfaces directly through the paints.

French Craqueler

This is a two part varnish and crackling medium which produces delicate cracks reminiscent of the surface of very old paintings. The Ageing Varnish, which is applied first, produces a mellowed antique look and gives a lovely golden colour to your finished piece. I have used Ageing Varnish and Cracking Varnish by Lefranc Bourgeois in the example.
1. Basecoat and decorate your piece as desired using your favourite brand of paint. I have used DecoArt™ Americana Sand in the example.
2. Using a large flat brush apply one even coat of Ageing Varnish.
3. When the Ageing Varnish is still wet but not sticky, apply a coat of Cracking Varnish using another large flat brush. To obtain large cracks, allow between 1 and 1½ hours before applying the Cracking Varnish. For smaller, finer cracks allow up to 3 hours maximum

Top coat brushed on — Top coat sponged on
Sandwich crackle (basecoat Sand, top coat Antique Gold)

Top coat crackle (basecoat Jo Sonja® Yellow Oxide, antiqued with Burnt Umber oil paint)

French Craqueler (basecoat DecoArt™ Sand, antiqued with Burnt Umber oil paint)

before applying the Cracking Varnish. The nature and degree of cracking depend greatly upon the temperature and the humidity in the air. If after one hour the cracks have not appeared, warm the surface with a hairdryer.
4. The 'cracked' appearance can be intensified by antiquing using an oil-based antiquing medium and oil paint. See Antiquing, page 26.
5. When the Cracking Varnish and/or antiquing has dried, apply one even coat of Ageing Varnish using a large flat brush.

ROCKING HORSE
Pattern on page 67

Worksheet for rocking horse—mane, eyelashes, circular roses and sponging

This the easiest beginner's piece and would make a lovely gift for new parents, commemorate one of baby's milestones or even a christening present. Change the basecoat colour to Pink Chiffon or French Mauve for a pretty pink for a little girl.

DecoArt™ Americana Acrylics
Winter Blue
Deep Midnight Blue
Williamsburg Blue
Buttermilk
Raspberry
Titanium White
Marigold

Brushes
size 3 Lea Davis Eco Fibre brush
size 10/0 Lea Davis Eco Fibre liner brush
size 8 or 10 flat brush for basecoating

Additional supplies
sea sponge
wooden satay skewer

Using the flat brush basecoat the surface with two coats of Winter Blue, sanding well between coats. Wipe over with a damp cloth to collect the sanding dust. Trace on the design for the saddle and bridle and roughly chalk in the area for the mane. You will find it easier to freehand in the designs on the legs and rocker.

Mane and tail Block in the area under the mane and tail with Williamsburg Blue using the flat brush. Don't take this colour down to the end of the mane, rather keep it confined to about 12 mm (½") from the edge. This will add depth under the mane so that the wispy hairs show up against the Winter Blue background colour. Load the liner brush in thinned Williamsburg Blue and start pulling down fine strokes. Keep working on this until you have enough hairs, then load the brush in Deep Midnight Blue and paint in some more. When you are satisfied that the mane and tail are nice and hairy, sideload the brush in Titanium White and place in a few final highlights.

Hooves Block in with two coats of Deep Midnight Blue

Saddle and bridle Block in the saddle with two coats of Buttermilk. Use the liner brush to paint the bridle with Buttermilk. Outline the bridle using Raspberry.

Eyelashes Again using the liner brush, paint the eyelashes with Deep Midnight Blue.

Sponging Moisten the sea sponge with water and wring out until quite dry. Dab the sponge up and down in a little Deep Midnight Blue and gently tap onto the surface around the saddle, down the legs and on the rockers. Pinch the sponge to make it smaller and use only light taps. You only need a hint of colour. Dry.

Roses Both colours of rose are painted the same way. Paint only three or four roses at a time as the paint dries too quickly to do more safely.

Pink roses: Using the size 3 brush paint a half circle of Raspberry. Apply quite a lot of paint. Wash the brush and using Titanium White paint the other half of the circle. Use the pointy end of the satay skewer to draw a circle through the two halves, thus making a complete circle. Start in the centre and spiral out. Don't overwork this step or you end up mixing the two colours together—usually once around is enough.

Yellow roses: Use Marigold and Titanium White and repeat the same steps.

Fillers Using your stylus or satay skewer place Titanium White dots randomly between the roses. Refer to the photograph or pattern for placement. Use the liner brush and Deep Midnight Blue to paint tiny sprigs peeking out from around the roses.

Varnish with your favourite varnish.

OVAL GARLAND BOX

Pattern on page 68

By the time you have finished this little box you will have perfected these roses!

DecoArt™ Americana Acrylics
Shale Green
Buttermilk
Dusty Rose
Light Buttermilk
Medium Flesh
Midnite Green
Red Iron Oxide

Brushes
sponge brush or 25 mm (1") flat brush for basecoating
size 3 or 5 Lea Davis Eco Fibre brush
10/0 Lea Davis Eco Fibre liner brush
size 6 or 8 flat brush

Additional supplies
synthetic sponge

Leaf Mix = Midnite Green + Shale Green [2:1]

Using the 25 mm (1") flat brush or the sponge brush, basecoat the lid with at least two coats of Shale Green, sanding lightly in between. Pay particular attention to the routed edges when sanding. On the base of the box the routed edge is painted Shale Green as well.

The sides of the box are painted in Buttermilk and you will need at least four coats, again sanding in be-

Worksheet for oval garland box—side design, leaves, fillers, dot flowers, and the steps in painting a rose

tween each coat. It is easier to paint the sides first and then go back and paint the routed edge using the flat brush. Mix the Leaf Mix with a little water to make a transparent wash. Pounce the sponge in this wash, tap the sponge onto a clean area of the palette to work the colour through, hold it against the side of the rim and drag it around the edge.

The inside of the box can be painted in the colour of your choice.

Trace on the pattern accurately.

Leaves Using the Leaf Mix, block in the leaves using the size 5 brush with at least two coats. Keep them nice and smooth with no ridges. Flatten the brush by sweeping the fibres through Light Buttermilk, then turn the brush onto the knife edge and place in the vein lines. Alternatively, use the Liner brush loaded in Light Buttermilk.

Roses The roses are alternately two colours, pink and apricot, both painted in the same way. They are indicated on the pattern by a 'p' for pink and an 'a' for apricot. You can use either the size 5 brush or the size 3—whatever you feel comfortable with.

Apricot roses Block in the circle with Medium Flesh and allow to dry. Recoat, and while this is still wet, pick up a little Red Iron Oxide on the tip of the brush and place a stroke down the left side of the rose. Tip the brush back into the Red Iron Oxide and paint a small circle at the centre top of the circle. Wipe the brush on paper towel, reload in Medium Flesh, sideload in Light Buttermilk and place in the petals around the back of the shaded circle. Sideload again in Light Buttermilk and place in the petals across the front of the rose. You can add a few extra strokes for variety if desired. Wipe the brush on paper towel, load again in Medium Flesh, sideload in Light Buttermilk and place in the comma stroke petals for the skirt. Add Light Buttermilk dots in the centre.

Pink roses Block in the circle with Dusty Rose. Recoat, and while this is still wet, pick up a little Red Iron Oxide on the tip of the brush and paint a small circle. Tip the brush back into Red Iron Oxide and place a stroke down the left side of the rose. Wipe the brush on paper towel, load again in Dusty Rose, sideload in Light Buttermilk and place in the petals around the shaded circle. Wipe the brush on paper towel, load again in Dusty Rose, sideload in Light Buttermilk and place in the comma stroke petals for the skirt. Add Light Buttermilk dots in the centre.

Fillers Paint comma strokes in the Leaf Mix, referring to the pattern for placement. Dip the handle of your paintbrush in Light Buttermilk and place five dots in a circle to make a tiny daisy.

Side design Mark off 2 cm (¾") intervals around the side of the box, 1 cm (³/₈") down from the top. Using the Leaf Mix and your liner brush paint a comma stroke border around the side. Add four tiny descending dots in between in either Medium Flesh or Dusty Rose.

Varnish with your favourite varnish.

LAP DESK AND PENCIL CADDY SET

Pattern on pages 69–70

DecoArt™ Americana Acrylics
Antique Gold
Antique Teal
Brandy Wine
Hauser Dark Green
Light Buttermilk

Brushes
size 5 Lea Davis Eco Fibre brush
size 3 Lea Davis Eco Fibre brush
10/0 Lea Davis Eco Fibre liner brush
25 mm (1″) flat brush for basecoating
size 6 or 8 flat brush

Lea Davis

Opposite: *Worksheet for lap desk and pencil caddy—steps in painting a tulip, hanging flowers, wood violets, poppies, leaves and the side design*
Above: *The four sides of the pencil caddy*

39

Using the flat brush basecoat the lid of the lap desk with at least two coats of Hauser Dark Green, sanding well between coats.

Paint the bottom of the desk with two coats of Brandy Wine, again sanding well between coats. Paint the routed edge with two coats of Antique Gold. You may find it easier to thin the paint slightly with water to help it flow when painting this area.

The pencil caddy is also basecoated in Hauser Dark Green, and the routed edge on the foot is Brandy Wine. Paint the cut edge along the top in Antique Gold and paint a fine Antique Gold line 5 mm (¼") down from the top.

Dry and trace on the patterns.

The painting instructions for the flowers are the same for both the lap desk and the pencil caddy.

Leaves (*Note* Wash leaves are indicated on the pattern by dotted lines.) All leaves are painted using the size 5 brush loaded in Antique Teal tipped in Antique Gold. Thin the paint with a little water and paint in the wash leaves. Don't paint the stems until the flowers are painted, as the flowers may not 'grow' exactly where the stems end.

Tulips Load the brush in Antique Gold, sideload in Brandy Wine and paint in the dark side of the tulip holding the Brandy Wine to the outside of the flower. Wipe the brush on paper towel, reload in Antique Gold, sideload in Light Buttermilk, and paint in the light side of the tulip holding the Light Buttermilk to the outside of the flower.

Sweep through a little more Light Buttermilk and holding the Light Buttermilk to the surface pull through the centre stroke to fill in the gap.

Poppies Starting at the back of the flower, sideload in Light Buttermilk and push out the back edge. Wipe the brush on paper towel, sweep through Brandy Wine and pull the Light Buttermilk down. Wipe the brush on paper towel, sideload in Light Buttermilk and linking up to the back, push off the Light Buttermilk across the front left side of the poppy. Wipe the brush on paper towel, sweep through Brandy Wine and pull the light Buttermilk down. Repeat for the other side. Using the tip of your liner brush paint dots inside the poppy in Antique Gold and Light Buttermilk, with a few dark ones in Hauser Dark Green.

Hanging flowers Load the brush in Brandy Wine, tip in Antique Gold and with the gold facing towards the surface paint the two bottom petals. Wipe the brush on paper towel, load in Antique Gold and tip in Light Buttermilk. Hold the Light Buttermilk to the surface and paint the two top petals. Add Light Buttermilk dots in the middle of the bottom two petals.

Wood violets Load the brush in Antique Gold and paint the back petal. Tip the brush in Light Buttermilk and paint the two side petals. Reload the brush in Antique Gold tip in Light Buttermilk and push up the front petal. Add a Burgundy Wine dot in the middle.

Stems Load the size 3 brush in Antique Teal and tip in Antique Gold. Hold the Antique Gold toward the surface and paint in the stems, reloading as often as necessary. You may like to touch the tip of the brush in a tiny drop of water to help the paint flow a little more easily. Use the liner brush for the very fine stems. Thin Antique Teal with a little water and load the liner brush right up to the ferrule. Sideload in Antique Gold and holding the gold toward the surface, paint the finer stems.

Band around stems Load the brush in Antique Gold and sideload in Light Buttermilk. Hold the Light Buttermilk to the inside and keeping up on the tip, paint two C-strokes around the stems.

Side design Measure down from the top of the sides 2 cm (¾") and draw a chalk line (A). Measure another 2 cm (¾") down from this line and draw another chalk line (C). Draw a line in the middle between the two (B). Load the liner brush in Antique Teal and tip in Light Buttermilk. Paint comma strokes 2 cm (¾") apart, starting on line A and going down to line B, all the way around the sides. Load the liner brush in Antique Gold and paint teardrops in between the commas, starting on line A and finishing on line C. Place a Light Buttermilk dot on the top of each teardrop.

Antique following the instructions on page 26 using Burnt Umber oil paint.

Varnish with your favourite oil compatible varnish.

Cheryl Bradshaw, a very dear friend and painter of beautiful Teddy Bears, gave me plain wooden pencils which I painted in matching colours. Being the wonderful friend she is, she also gave me matching tassels which I glued to the top of each pencil.

GARDEN SET

Pattern on page 71

Garden set of gloves and plant pot

Worksheet for garden set—rim design for the pot, leaves, daisies, bow and filler flowers, and the rose and filler flowers for the gloves

I have painted the gloves and the Patio Paint pot in different colours to give you a wider choice. They would look wonderful painted as a matching set as a special gift for an avid gardener.

GARDENING GLOVES

DecoArt™ Americana Acrylics
Hauser Dark Green
Titanium White
Deep Burgundy
Raspberry
Marigold
Sapphire

Brushes
size 3 Lea Davis Eco Fibre brush
size 10/0 Lea Davis Eco Fibre liner brush

Additional supplies
sea sponge
DecoArt™ Americana Fabric Painting Medium

Wash and dry the gloves (don't use fabric softener) and iron out the creases. Place cardboard shapes inside the gloves to stop the paint from seeping through to the other side. Cut-up milk cartons are ideal for this.

You will need to mix each colour with Fabric Painting Medium [2 parts paint to 1 part medium] on a dry palette before you start painting.

Moisten the sea sponge and wring out until quite dry. Dab into Hauser Dark Green and sponge the area on the back of the gloves underneath the design. Dry and trace on the pattern.

Roses Block in the circle with two coats of Raspberry using the size 3 round brush. When dry, load the liner brush in Deep Burgundy and place lines across the left side of the rose, following the shape of the circle and leaving a plain circle at the top. Repeat on the other side, using Titanium White. Load the brush in Raspberry, sideload in Titanium White and paint the petals around the rose—all you need to do is just press the brush down and lift off. Paint tiny Titanium White dots in the centre.

Leaves Block in the shape with Hauser Dark Green. Dry and recoat if necessary. Add veins using the liner brush and Titanium White. Casually outline the leaves with Deep Burgundy.

Filler flowers Load the brush in Marigold, tip in Titanium White and 'dab' the flowers in. Place dots in a circle of five or a group of three in Sapphire, Raspberry and Hauser Dark Green.

Dry the gloves for 24 to 48 hours. Place a soft cloth over the design and dry heat set for a minimum of 30 seconds.

PATIO PAINT POT

DecoArt™ Patio Paint is a fantastic acrylic paint which is permanent and weatherproof and is suitable for concrete, terracotta and wood. It will not crack or peel and is fade resistant and lightfast. Now you can colour coordinate all your garden pots and statuary!

DecoArt™ Patio Paint™
Pine Green
Cloud White
Daisy Cream
Fern Green
Sunflower Yellow
Woodland Brown

Brushes
sponge brush
size 5 Lea Davis Eco Fibre brush
10/0 Lea Davis Eco Fibre liner brush

Using the sponge brush and Pine Green, basecoat the pot and saucer with three or four coats. You will find this paint 'slips' on so there is no need to sand between coats. When dry, trace on the pattern.

Leaves Block in with two coats of Fern Green. Wipe the brush on paper towel, load in Daisy Cream and paint in the strokes on the leaves. Alternatively, use the liner brush.

Daisies Load the size 5 brush in Daisy Cream and paint in the petals. Wash the brush, load in Sunflower Yellow and tap in the centres. Wash the brush, load in Cloud White and place in a smaller stroke than the previous one on the front three or four petals. Using the tip of your liner brush or a fine-pointed stylus, dip into Woodland Brown and place dots along the bottom of the daisy centre.

Wipe the point, dip into Cloud White and place dots all around the centre—you will need to reload frequently. The daisy buds have a Cloud White dot where the petals join onto the stem.

Stems Load the liner brush with Fern Green and paint all the stems.

Bow Load the size 5 brush in Sunflower Yellow and tip in Cloud White. Paint the loops on either side first, then finish off with the knot.

Fillers Add comma strokes in Fern Green. Place in dots in Cloud White.

Rim design Load the liner brush in Woodland Brown, tip in Cloud White and paint in the branches. Paint in the leaves with the size 5 brush tipped in Cloud White. Add dots of Cloud White.

FAUX FINISH COASTER BOX WITH PEONIES

Illustrated on page 6
Pattern on page 72

DecoArt™ Americana Acrylics
Red Iron Oxide
Antique Gold Deep
Antique Green
Brandy Wine
French Mocha
Lamp (Ebony) Black
Light Buttermilk
Midnite Blue

Brushes
25 mm (1") flat brush for basecoating
size 3 or 5 Lea Davis Eco Fibre brush
10/0 Lea Davis Eco Fibre liner brush

Additional supplies
DecoArt™ Americana Acrylic Sealer/Finisher (matte)
DecoArt™ Gel Stain in Walnut
greaseproof paper
Jo Sonja® Tannin Blocking Sealer for Wood
imitation gold leaf (Dutch metal)
cotton gloves (for applying the gold leaf)

Using the flat brush basecoat the box inside and out, and all the coasters, with at least two coats of Red Iron Oxide, sanding well between coats. Collect the sanding dust with a damp cloth.

Gilded coasters Apply Tannin Blocking Sealer to the four coasters to be gilded and allow to touch dry. Apply one more smooth even coat and allow to touch dry. Put on the cotton gloves and pick up a sheet of gold leaf. Press it onto the surface of one of the coasters you have just tannin-blocked. Smooth it out carefully—I like my gold leaf to have cracks in it so the base colour shows through, but the choice is yours. Repeat with the remaining three coasters. Spray lightly with matte Sealer/Finisher.

Faux finish coasters and coaster holder Tear greaseproof paper into manageable sections (about A4 size works for me). You will need one piece for each coaster and pieces for the lid and bottom of the coaster holder. Working one coaster or surface at a time, use the 25 mm (1") flat brush to apply the Gel Stain™ evenly over the area. Take a section of greaseproof paper and loosely crumple it in your palm. Pat this over the surface. Keep turning the paper around in your hand to a dry area as you move across the surface. That's it! Allow to dry.

Trace on the pattern for the lid and sides of the coaster holder.

Leaves Using the size 3 or 5 brush, mix a little Lamp Black into Antique Green to make a dark green and block in the leaves. You will need two coats. Sweep the dirty brush through Antique Gold Deep, then through a little Light Buttermilk. Turn the brush onto the knife edge and paint in the vein lines. The comma strokes around the design are painted with the brush loaded in this way as well.

Peonies Load the brush in Red Iron Oxide and tip in Antique Gold Deep. Tap in the centre of the flower, being careful not to blend the two colours together. Wipe the brush on paper towel, load in French Mocha, sideload in Light Buttermilk and holding the Light Buttermilk to the inside of the flower, paint in the tiny comma strokes across the back. Reload the brush in the same way and place in the strokes across the front of the flower, starting with the ones on the outside. Hold the Light Buttermilk to the inside and reload for each stroke. For the centre stroke, hold the Light Buttermilk to the surface and pull through. Wipe the brush on paper towel, sideload in Light Buttermilk and push out the skirt, starting at the back. Wipe the brush on paper towel, sweep through French Mocha and pull the white down. Repeat

Worksheet for coaster set—steps in painting the peony, leaves, fillers and blue daisies on the faux finish background

the same technique all the way around the skirt. I find it easier to work from side to side and then turn my work upside down and finish off with the front petal.

Blue daisies Load the tip of the brush in Midnite Blue and 'dance' the tip up and down in Light Buttermilk. Gently place the tip of the brush down and paint five little petals in a circle to make a daisy. Load the brush in Antique Gold Deep, sideload in Light Buttermilk and touch the tip into the middle of each daisy for the centre.

Side design Load the liner brush in the leaf mix, sweep through Antique Gold Deep, sweep through Light Buttermilk and paint the long S-strokes around the side. Change to the size 3 brush and with the same brush loading as before, paint the graduating comma strokes up either side of the S-stroke.

Antique with Burnt Umber oil paint and allow to dry for at least four days before varnishing with your favourite oil-compatible varnish.

DINNER CATS

Patterns on pages 72–74

This placemat and coaster set is great fun to paint and so easy—a great gift for a pussy cat lover. The design could be adapted to other articles such as boxes and photograph frames.

There is no colour worksheet for this project as the cats are so easy to paint.

DecoArt™ Americana Acrylics
Antique White
Antique Gold
Dove Grey
Lamp (Ebony) Black
Light Cinnamon

Rookwood Red
Titanium White
Williamsburg Blue

Brushes
size 8 flat brush
size 3 Lea Davis Eco Fibre brush
size 10/0 Lea Davis Eco Fibre liner brush
size 1/8 deerfoot stippler
sponge brush for basecoating

Additional supplies
Scotties Antiquing Patina Medium
Burnt Umber oil paint
cotton buds

Using the sponge brush and Antique White, basecoat the mat and coasters with at least five coats of Antique White, sanding well between coats. When dry, sand very well once again and transfer the pattern using light pressure. Thin Rookwood Red with water to the consistency of ink and using the liner brush carefully paint the line. Dry and trace on the pussy cats, making certain they sit just on the line. The pussy cats are numbered on the pattern. There are three basic shapes with a variation in markings for each one.

Block in each shape until opaque, dry, then reapply the pattern for the details. The features are painted the same way for each pussy cat after the body shapes have dried, and the shading done later with selective antiquing (see page 27).

Pussy cat 1 Block in with Dove Grey. Using the deerfoot stippler and Titanium White, stipple in the white patch on the face and chest. Block in the tail with Ebony Black. Using the round brush, paint the markings and the fringe with Lamp Black. Outline the head, leg and chest, again using Lamp Black.

OPPOSITE: *Dinner cats placemat and coasters meet with Charlie's approval!*

Pussy cat 2 Block in using Antique Gold. Outline the head and legs with a mix of Antique Gold + Ebony Black. This colour should be a dark green. Pounce the deerfoot stippler in a Little Light Cinnamon, pounce again on a dry area of the palette, and place in the markings. Dry off the brush on paper towel, then pounce in a little Titanium White and stipple this on top of the Light Cinnamon. Keep the markings light and airy. The bird is blocked in with Rookwood Red and outlined in Ebony Black. Paint a tiny dot of Titanium White for the eye. The legs are also Ebony Black.

Pussy cat 3 Block in with Light Cinnamon. Using the deerfoot stippler and Titanium White stipple in the patch on the face. Paint the tip of the tail using Titanium White and the size 3 round brush. Outline the face, legs and tail with Titanium White using the liner brush.

Pussy cat 4 Block in with Antique Gold. Using the deerfoot stippler, stipple the patch on the face with Titanium White. Block in the tail using the round brush and Titanium White. Mix a little Antique Gold + Ebony Black and use this dark green mix to outline the face, tail and leg. Pounce the stippler in a little Light Cinnamon and stipple the markings. Wipe the brush on paper towel, tap into a little Titanium White and pounce this colour next to the Light Cinnamon patches. Keep them light and airy. Block in the bird with Ebony Black and paint a tiny Titanium White dot for his eye. His legs are Ebony Black.

Pussy cat 6 Block in with Antique Gold. Mix a little Antique Gold + Ebony Black to make a dark green and using the liner brush, outline the face, tail and legs with this mix. The markings are Ebony Black. The bird is painted with Rookwood Red and has a tiny Titanium White dot for his eye. His legs are Ebony Black.

COASTERS

Pussy cat 7 Block in with Antique Gold. Block in the tip of the tail and the inside of the ears with Light Cinnamon using the size 3 brush. Outline the body, face and legs with Light Cinnamon. Using the deerfoot stippler, stipple on the markings on the face and chest using Light Cinnamon. Fade the colour off on the chest as you move towards the legs by wiping the stippler on paper towel and working the dryer paint down.

Pussy cat 5 Block in with Ebony Black. Using the deerfoot stippler, stipple in the patches on the face and chest with Titanium White. Block in the tip on the tail and the inside of the ears with Titanium White. Outline the legs with white also, using the liner brush.

Pussy cat 8 Block in with Dove Grey. Outline the head, body, legs and tail with Ebony Black. The markings and fringe are Ebony Black also.

Pussy cat 10 Block in with Light Cinnamon. Using the deerfoot stippler, stipple in the patches on the face and body with Titanium White. Paint the tip of the tail with Titanium White using the round brush, and outline the head and legs with Titanium White also. The bird is Ebony Black with Ebony Black legs as well. He has a tiny Titanium White dot for his eye.

Pussy cat 9 Block in with Ebony Black. Using the deerfoot stippler, stipple in the patches on the face and body with Dove Grey. Touch the stippler in a little Titanium White and stipple on a smaller patch next to the grey ones, keeping the markings light and airy. Outline the head, legs and tail with Titanium White. The bird is Antique Gold outlined in Ebony Black, with Ebony Black legs.

Cats' faces

Eyes Paint two tiny dots in Lamp Black with a stylus or the point of a ballpoint pen. When dry, paint in smaller dots using Titanium White, one above each eye and one below.

Nose Block in with Ebony Black using the size 3 brush. Paint a Titanium White highlight across the top of the nose using the liner brush.

Mouth Paint fine lines using Lamp Black.

Blush on cheeks Tap a cotton bud in Rookwood Red, tap onto a clean area of the palette to work the colour into the cotton, then dab up and down in a circle on each cheek. Keep the edges soft and uneven.

Whiskers Lamp Black, again using the liner brush.

Leave overnight to dry before antiquing with Burnt Umber oil paint following the directions for antiquing and selective antiquing on pages 26–27.

When dry varnish with at least four coats of varnish, preferably more for added protection.

THREE PAPIER-MÂCHÉ DAISY BOXES

Patterns on page 75

I love painting these boxes, illustrated below, as special gifts for my friends and loved ones. They are quick work and quite inexpensive, so you should be able to paint lots of them.

OVAL BOX

DecoArt™ Americana Acrylics
Blue Haze
Burgundy Wine
Ice Blue
Light Buttermilk
Moon Yellow
Wood Sealer

Brushes
size 3 Lea Davis Eco Fibre brush
10/0 Lea Davis Eco Fibre liner brush
sponge brush

Background Mix = Ice Blue + Blue Haze [3:1]

Using the sponge brush coat the box inside and out with one coat of Wood Sealer. When dry basecoat the box inside and out with two coats of Background Mix. Dry and apply the pattern.

Leaves Block in with two coats of Blue Haze. Using the dirty brush sweep through Light Buttermilk and paint the veins on the leaves. You can use your liner brush for this if you prefer.

Worksheet for daisy boxes—from the top, the ribbon for the heart box, the daisies for the oval box, the octagonal box and the heart box, and fillers in Glorious Gold

Daisies (top row of worksheet) Load the size 3 brush in Light Buttermilk and paint the petals. Two strokes make up each petal. Add a Burgundy Wine dot in the centre.

Fillers Paint little comma strokes in groups of two using Moon Yellow. Add tiny dots in a circle of five with Light Buttermilk.

Side design Measure up approximately 5 mm (¼") from the bottom of the box and draw a chalk line around the box. Paint the comma stroke leaves in Blue Haze and the little daisies in Light Buttermilk.

Varnish with your favourite varnish.

OCTAGONAL BOX

DecoArt™ Americana Acrylics
Antique Gold Deep
Burgundy Wine
Deep Midnight Blue
Light Buttermilk
Williamsburg Blue
Wood Sealer

Brushes
size 3 Lea Davis Eco Fibre brush
size 10/0 Lea Davis Eco Fibre liner brush
sponge brush

Using the sponge brush coat the box inside and out with the Wood Sealer. When dry basecoat all surfaces with two coats of Williamsburg Blue. Trace on the pattern.

Leaves Block in the leaves with two coats of Deep Midnight Blue. Load the liner brush in Light Buttermilk and paint in the veins. Use this brush to paint the stems in deep Midnight Blue. Change to the size 3 brush and paint the tiny commas along the stems.

Daisies (middle row of worksheet) Start with the two underneath daisies and work one petal at a time. Push out the edge in Light Buttermilk, wipe the brush on the paper towel, sweep through Antique Gold Deep and pull the Light Buttermilk down. Repeat for all the daisy petals. For the centre, tap in a little circle of Antique Gold Deep. While this is still wet, tap Burgundy Wine across one side and Light Buttermilk across the other. Soften into the Antique Gold Deep by tapping the line where the two colours meet.

Buds Load the brush in Burgundy Wine, tip in Light Buttermilk and holding the Light Buttermilk to the surface, paint a blob. Add a Light Buttermilk dot where the bud joins the stem.

Fillers Paint five tiny dots in a circle in Light Buttermilk.

Side design Chalk a line 1 cm ($^3/_8$″) up from the bottom of the box. Use the liner brush loaded in Deep Midnight Blue then sideloaded in Light Buttermilk to paint S-strokes across each panel.

Varnish with your favourite varnish.

HEART BOX

DecoArt™ Americana Acrylics
Burgundy Wine
Deep Midnight Blue
French Mauve
Light Buttermilk
Uniform Blue
Wood Sealer

DecoArt™ Dazzling Metallics
Glorious Gold

Brushes
size 3 Lea Davis Eco Fibre brush
size 10/0 Lea Davis Eco Fibre brush
sponge brush

Additional supplies
sea sponge

Using the sponge brush basecoat the box inside and out with one coat of Wood Sealer. Dry, and using the same brush, apply two coats of Deep Midnight Blue. Dry. Moisten the sea sponge with water and wring out until quite dry. Mix together Uniform Blue + Light Buttermilk [4:1], add a little water and pounce the sea sponge up and down in this mix. Pounce off the excess colour on paper towel then sponge the lid. Keep the effect subdued. Dry. Trace on the pattern.

Leaves Block in the leaves with Uniform Blue using the size 3 round brush. Mix a little Light Buttermilk into Uniform Blue to lighten the colour and casually outline the leaves with this using the liner brush. Load the liner brush in this mix, sideload in Light Buttermilk and place in the veins on the leaves.

Ribbon *On the lid* Load size 3 brush in Uniform Blue, sideload in Light Buttermilk and, holding the Light Buttermilk to the outside of the ribbon, use pressure to create width.

On the side Load the same brush in French Mauve, sideload in Light Buttermilk and again use pressure to create width, decreasing pressure and lifting up on the fibres to make a finer line. Flip the Light Buttermilk edge of the brush from side to side to create a twist in the ribbon.

Daisies (bottom row on worksheet) Load the round brush in French Mauve, tip in Light Buttermilk; hold the Light Buttermilk to the surface and place in the back petals. Wipe the brush on paper towel, load the brush in French Mauve and this time sideload in Light Buttermilk. Hold the Light Buttermilk towards the centre and paint the petals across the front. Place a Burgundy Wine dot in the centre with a smaller Glorious Gold dot on top of that.

Fillers Paint Glorious Gold sprigs around the design. Add five tiny dots in a circle on top of the leaves.

Varnish with your favourite varnish.

ROSES HEART BOX
Pattern on page 76

DecoArt™ Americana Acrylics
Antique Mauve
Warm Neutral
Cranberry Wine
Light Buttermilk
Mauve

Midnite Blue
Williamsburg Blue

DecoArt™ Dazzling Metallics
Royal Ruby
White Pearl

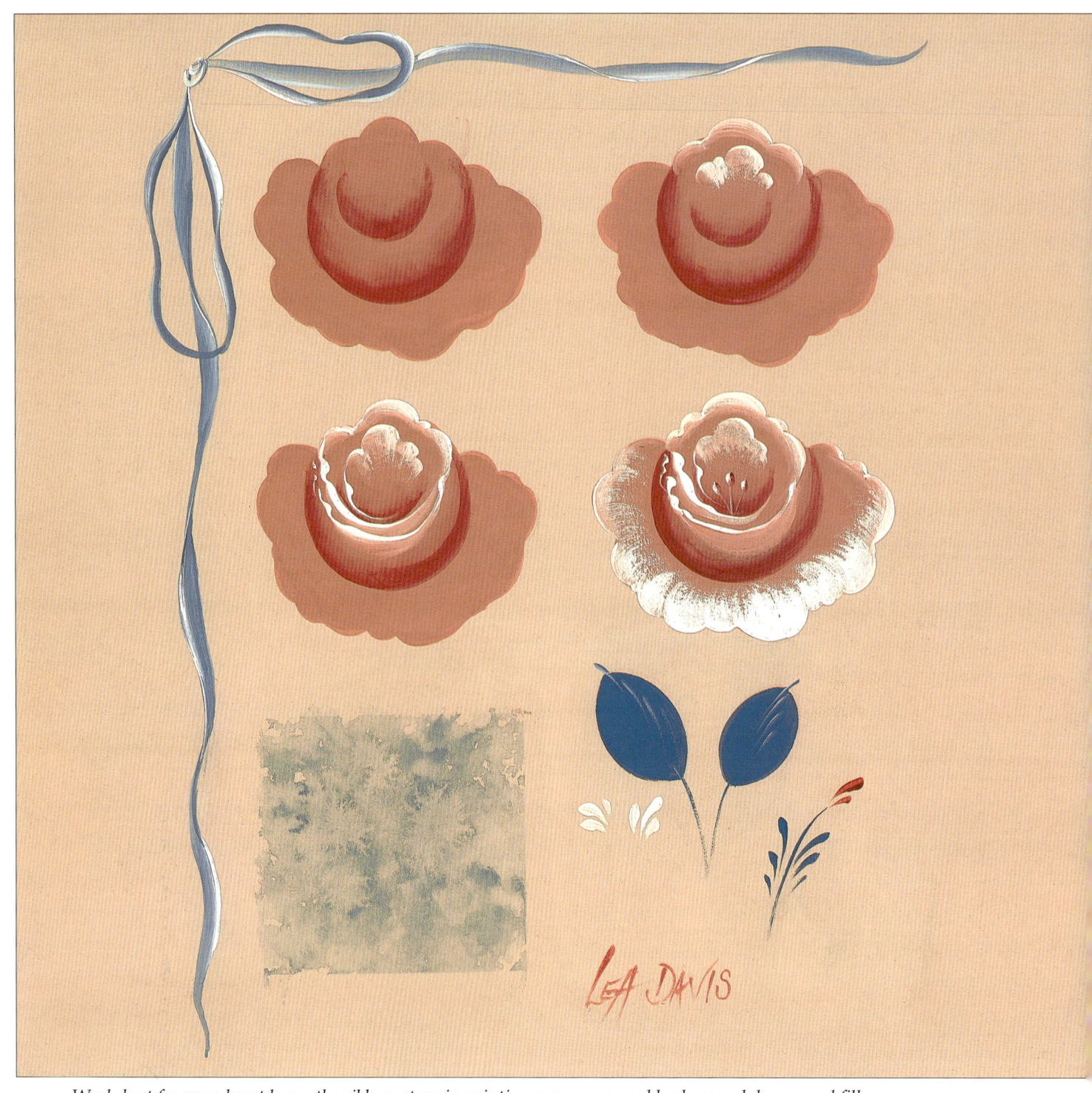

Worksheet for roses heart box—the ribbon, steps in painting a rose, sponged background, leaves and fillers

Brushes
sponge brush or 25 mm (1") flat brush Size 3 or 5 Lea Davis Eco Fibre brush
size 10/0 Lea Davis Eco Fibre liner brush
size 6 or 8 flat brush

Additional supplies
plastic wrap
sea sponge

Leaf Mix = Midnite Blue + Williamsburg Blue [2:1]

Using either the flat brush or the sponge brush, basecoat the surface with at least two coats of Warm Neutral, sanding well between coats. Moisten the sea sponge with water and wring out until quite dry. Mix the Leaf Mix with a little water to make a transparent colour. Tap the sponge into the watery Leaf Mix, pounce on a clean area of the palette and gently tap onto the lid of the box, keeping the colour about 3 cm (1¼") in from the edge. The colour should be soft and muted, so add more water if it is too dark. Dry and trace on the pattern.

CONTINUED ON PAGE **57**

PANSY TEAPOT AND SUGAR BOWL

Patterns on page 76

These pieces with their cheerful pansies and gold crackled areas make a fun setting; they would look great holding your teabags and teaspoons at an afternoon tea with friends. Bill and Mary from Walla Walla cut out the shapes for my dear friend Carolyn and she kindly gave me a set.

DecoArt™ Americana Acrylics
Sand
Avocado
Light Buttermilk
Cadmium Yellow
Dioxazine Purple
Glorious Gold
Pansy Lavender
Plantation Pine
Violet Haze

Brushes
sponge brush or 25 mm (1") flat brush for basecoating
size 3 Lea Davis Eco Fibre brush
10/0 Lea Davis Eco Fibre liner brush
size 8 flat brush

Additional supplies
DecoArt™ Weathered Wood
sea sponge

Using the flat brush or the sponge brush, basecoat the pieces (excluding the insides of the boxes) with two coats of Sand, sanding well between coats. Paint inside the boxes with two coats of Pansy Lavender.

Crackling Place the patterns over the shapes and draw chalk marks on two or three areas outside the designs. These are the areas that you will be crackling so you don't want them underneath your painting. Paint patches of Glorious Gold where the chalk marks are, keeping the edges ragged and uneven, using the flat brush. When this is dry, paint over the same patches with the Weathered Wood, using the same brush. Allow this to dry. Moisten the sea sponge with water and wring out until almost dry. Pounce the sponge in Sand and sponge over the Weathered Wood, being careful not to overwork. Make sure the sponge has plenty of paint in it before you start on your piece. The cracks should start to appear in a few seconds. Allow to dry, then trace on the patterns.

Worksheet for pansies—steps in painting a pansy, snowdrops, leaves and antiquing over Glorious Gold

Leaves Block in the large leaves with two coats of Avocado, using the size 3 round brush. Wipe off the excess paint on paper towel, load the brush in Light Buttermilk and, keeping up on the tip of the brush, place in the vein lines on the leaves. Alternatively, use the liner brush loaded in Light Buttermilk. Paint the stems and tendrils using the liner brush and Plantation Pine. The smaller leaves are painted with the round brush loaded in Avocado and tipped in Plantation Pine. Try and paint them using one stroke for each leaf.

Pansies Refresh your memory of the pull-in technique by going back to page 21. I have painted each pansy using three colours, but you may prefer to paint them using only one colour. Please refer to the step by step worksheet as you read the instructions.
Pansy 1:
   Back two petals—Violet Haze
   Middle two petals—Pansy Lavender
   Front petal—Dioxazine Purple

Pansy 2 and the pansy on the sugar bowl:
  Back two petals—Dioxazine Purple
  Middle two petals—Violet Haze
  Front petal—Pansy Lavender

The method of painting the pansies is the same for three. Use the size 3 round brush and remember to pull your strokes in towards the centre.

Starting with the back petals, sideload the brush in Light Buttermilk and push out the edge. Wipe the brush on paper towel, sweep through the back petal colour and pull the white down. Wipe the brush on paper towel, sideload in Light Buttermilk and push out the middle petals. Wipe the brush on paper towel, sweep through the middle petal colour and pull the white edge down.

Turn your work upside down to paint the front petal. Wipe the brush, sideload in Light Buttermilk and push out the edge on the front petal, wipe the brush, sweep through the front petal colour and pull the white edge down. The pansy buds are painted the same way.

Now mix a little Plantation Pine into Dioxazine Purple to make a dark purple. Using your liner brush, place in the lines on the front and middle petals, pulling them into the centre. Place a Cadmium Yellow dot in the centre.

Snowdrops These are so easy and are such fun. Work only two or three at a time. Paint a circle using lots of paint, keeping the circles smaller nearer the tip of the stem. Working quickly, take your stylus or empty ball-point pen and pull out three little petals for each ball. That's it!

Gold linework Using the liner brush and Glorious Gold paint all the lines around spout, handle and lids.

I decided not to antique my pieces but I think they would look terrific if you did. Follow the instructions on page 26 if you would like to.

Varnish with the appropriate varnish.

ROSES HEART BOX instructions continued from page 54

Ribbon Load the size 5 brush in Williamsburg Blue and sideload in Light Buttermilk. Work the colours together a little on your palette by stroking the brush back and forwards a few times to softly blend them. Starting on the tip of the brush, apply pressure to create width where needed. Reload the brush as often as necessary. Dry.

Leaves Use the same brush as before and block in the leaves with the Leaf Mix, making certain that the there are no ridges. Using the dirty brush, sweep through Light Buttermilk, turn the brush onto the knife edge and paint in the vein lines.

Roses Block in all three roses with two coats of Mauve. Reapply the pattern for the roses using the chalk method (see page 13). Wash Antique Mauve around the bowl of the rose (the outer ring). Dry and apply again if you think the colour is not deep enough. Wash in the centre shaded area with Cranberry Wine, again washing in more colour if needed. Load the brush in Mauve, sideload in Light Buttermilk and push out the edges around the centre starting along the back of the rose. Move around to the front of the centre and repeat. Wash the brush, load in Light Buttermilk, wipe off the excess on paper towel, and dry brush the white highlight on the skirt of the rose. You will need to apply a few layers to build up the opacity. Load the liner brush in Light Buttermilk, sideload in Cranberry Wine and place in the stamens.

Fillers You can use either the size 3 brush or the liner brush for these. The stems and leaves are painted in Leaf Mix and the little flowers are Cranberry Wine. Add a few extra flowers in Light Buttermilk. Keep these small.

Sides Mix Light Buttermilk with water (approximately 1 part paint to 2 parts water) and apply to the sides of the box using the large flat brush or the sponge brush. Tear off a large piece of plastic wrap and apply it to the wet paint. Lift off carefully. If you don't like the pattern, paint again and apply more plastic wrap. When you are satisfied, allow to dry. Wipe off any spills with a cotton bud.

Routed edge Mix Royal Ruby + White Pearl [1:1]. Thin slightly with a little water and paint the routed edge around the lid and bottom using the flat brush.

Varnish with your favourite varnish.

TISSUE BOX COVER AND PICTURE FRAME

Pattern on page 77

Decorating plain articles with latex mouldings is so easy to do and great fun. You can choose from a wide range of mouldings to create individual pieces. You don't have to use the same mouldings that I used here.

DecoArt™ Americana Acrylics
Asphaltum

DecoArt™ Dazzling Metallics
Venetian Gold
Emperor's Gold

DecoArt™ Heavenly Hues
Patina Green

Brushes
25 mm (1") flat brush
size 3 Lea Davis Eco Fibre brush

Additional supplies
decorative latex mouldings (see stockist list, page 80)
tissue box: moulding strip cc327 in the length required
picture frame: moulding cc63, swag med X2; moulding

Step 1—base in Asphaltum

Step 2—sponge on Venetian Gold

Step 3—sponge on Emperor's Gold

Step 4—sponge on Patina Green and paint scrolls

cc91, button rosette; moulding cc595, cherub
Selleys Kwik Grip contact adhesive, 100 ml tube
sea sponge

Position the latex mouldings on the picture frame, making certain they are even, and mark their positions with a pencil. Measure and cut the correct length of strip moulding for the tissue box cover. Draw a line 2 cm (¾") up from the bottom of the box.

Following the instructions on the tube, apply the Selleys Kwik Grip glue to the backs of the mouldings, coating only the raised edges (don't try and fill in the hollows). Allow about 20 minutes for the glue to dry, then press on the mouldings following your pencil guidelines. Easy! If the edges lift anywhere, simply use an old brush to push a little more glue underneath the raised spot, wait for the glue to dry and stick down again. Allow the glue to dry for a few hours. Using the flat brush basecoat the surfaces (including the mouldings) with two coats of Asphaltum, sanding the wooden surfaces well between coats.

Squeeze out a puddle of Venetian Gold on a dry palette. Moisten the sea sponge with water and tap into a little of the paint. Move onto a clean area of the palette and pounce the sponge up and down to distribute the paint evenly. Tap the sponge lightly over the surface of your pieces, turning it constantly so as to avoid creating a repeating pattern. Don't try and cover the surface with paint—rather, allow the brown to show through.

Don't wash out the sponge. Squeeze out a puddle of Emperor's Gold and repeat the sponging procedure. Allow the pieces to dry. Wash out the sponge and squeeze out the excess water.

Pour out a puddle of Heavenly Hues Patina Green. Working on one piece at a time and using the flat brush, coat the entire surface with Patina Green. While the paint is still wet, use the slightly damp sea sponge to remove the excess paint from the mouldings, allowing the colour to remain in the crevices and hollows. Wash the sponge out frequently. On the top of the tissue box, I dragged the sponge from one end to the other, creating even lines. On the picture frame, however, I tapped the sponge up and down to soften and mottle the surface. Try both ways and see which one you like best. If you wipe off too much colour, reapply and wipe off again. Allow to dry.

Scrolls Apply the pattern to the tissue box. Load the size 3 brush in either Venetian Gold or Emperor's Gold and paint in the scrolls, tipping into either one of the golds as required.

Dry and remove any tracing lines. Varnish with at least three coats of varnish.

WILDFLOWER BOX

Pattern on page 78

DecoArt™ Americana Acrylics
Antique Gold Deep
Antique Green
Black Green
Burnt Umber
Cadmium Yellow
Calico Red
Raw Sienna
Titanium (Snow) White

Brushes
size 3 Lea Davis Eco Fibre brush
Size 10/0 Lea Davis Eco Fibre liner brush
25 mm (1") flat brush or sponge brush
small deerfoot stippler

Using the flat brush or the sponge brush, basecoat the box inside and out with two coats of Black Green, sanding well between coats. Trace on the pattern.

Leaves Mix a little Burnt Umber into Antique Green to slightly dull and darken the green and block in the banksia leaves. Add a little Titanium White to this mix and outline each leaf. You will need to thin the paint

Banksia flower

Flannel flower

Desert baeckea

Snow daisy

Wattle

Gum blossom

61

with a little water to help it flow. Use this mix to paint in the stems also. All other leaves, except the flannel flower leaves, are Antique Green outlined in Antique Green + Titanium White. Again, reduce the consistency of the paint with a little water. For the tiny flannel flower leaves load the brush in Titanium White, tip in Black Green, and paint in.

Banksia flower Block in the flowerhead with two coats of Raw Sienna. Mix a little Titanium White into the Raw Sienna and pull some wispy lines with your liner brush over the Raw Sienna. Load the liner brush in thick Titanium White and starting at the top, pull little comma strokes all over the body of the flower. As you near the base of the flowerhead pull them in towards the stem. Block in the stem and the calyx with Raw Sienna + a little Titanium White. Using the liner brush and Burnt Umber, paint fine criss-cross lines across the calyx. Thin Raw Sienna with a little water and wash a shadow down either side of the flowerhead, leaving the middle as a highlight.

Flannel flower There are two layers of petals—a dark layer and a light layer. For the dark layer, load the brush in Black Green and tip in a little Titanium White. Start at the tip and paint in all the underneath petals (marked on the pattern with a *). For the light layer, load the brush in Titanium White and sideload in Black Green. Starting at the tip and holding the Black Green towards the centre, paint one side of the petal. Start at the tip again and paint the other side. Two strokes make one petal. Tap Titanium White in the centre of the flower; while this is still wet tap a little Black Green across the bottom and blend the two colours together by tapping them gently.

Desert baeckea Load the brush in Titanium White and paint in each of the petals. When dry paint a smaller stroke in the middle of each petal as a highlight. With the dirty brush, tip in a little Calico Red and tap into the centre. Place Calico Red dots around the centre.

Gum blossom Block in the gumnut with Burnt Umber and while this is still wet, blend a little Titanium White on the right side as a highlight. When this is dry, add a smaller stroke of Titanium White in the same area for a stronger highlight. Using the liner brush paint fine lines of Calico Red for the 'petals'. Keep working on the lines to build up the colour. Add a little Titanium White to the brush and add more lines with this colour. You may need to reduce the consistency of the paint by adding a little water. This will help you pull finer lines. Add tiny dots of Antique Gold Deep using the tip of the liner brush, then using the same brush pick up a little Titanium White and add a few more dots.

Snow daisy Pull all the petals in towards the centre using Titanium White. Tap Antique Green into the centre. Load the tip of the brush in Antique Gold Deep and sideload in Titanium White. Hold the brush low to the surface and tap around the centre, aiming to create an elongated stroke. Reduce the pressure as you move around to the back of the centre.

Wattle There are three layers of blossoms—dark, medium and light. You need only paint a few blossoms for each layer—any more and the wattle looks too heavy.

For each layer load the deerfoot stippler in the required colour, pushing the paint into the bristles, then tap the excess off onto paper towel.

First layer (dark) Load the brush in Antique Gold Deep and tap in a few blossoms.

Second layer (medium) Use the dirty brush from the first layer and touch into a little Cadmium Yellow. Tap in a few more blossoms.

Third layer (light) Again, use the dirty brush from before. Touch into a little more Cadmium Yellow and then into a little Titanium White. Pounce the two together on your palette and place in a few more blossoms.

Side design Paint the curving stem first using the same colours as for the stems on the top of the box. The pattern can be lengthened by repeating the design to fit the dimensions of your piece. The flowers are painted the same way as those on the lid.

Varnish with your favourite varnish.

BLUE BOWL
Pattern on page 79

tulip

daisies

morning glory

little daisy   *snowdrops*

fuchsia   *fillers*

wash leaves

Lea Davis ©1998

This beautiful bowl was turned by my very dear friends from Craft Turn, Kath and Paul Richards. Paul turns all kinds of wonderful things so keep an eye out in your local art and craft shop for more of his designs.

Please refresh your memory of the criss-cross background technique on page 25 before painting this piece.

DecoArt™ Americana Acrylics
Light Buttermilk
Williamsburg Blue
Titanium White
Antique Gold
Deep Midnight Blue
Marigold
Raw Sienna
Red Iron Oxide
True Ochre
Yellow Ochre

Brushes
25 mm (1") flat bristle brush (a stiff inexpensive brush available from art and craft shops)
size 3 Lea Davis Eco Fibre brush
size 10/0 Lea Davis Eco Fibre liner brush

Leaf Mix = Deep Midnight Blue + Raw Sienna [3:1]

Using Light Buttermilk, Williamsburg Blue and Titanium White, follow the instructions for the criss-cross background technique to basecoat the bowl inside and out. When dry, sand lightly and wipe over with a damp cloth to collect the dust. Trace on the pattern.

Leaves Using the size 3 brush block in the leaves with the Leaf Mix. Dry and recoat. Paint the stems on the leaves (don't do the flower stems just yet) using this same mix and the liner brush. Load the liner brush in the Leaf Mix, sideload in Light Buttermilk and paint the veins on the leaves.

The tulip leaf is painted differently. Load the size 3 brush in Leaf Mix, sideload in Antique Gold and starting at the tip with light pressure, paint the leaf. Increase pressure to create width in the leaf and flip the brush from one side to the other to create the twist.

Don't paint the wash leaves yet.

Tulip The painting sequence for the petals is marked on the pattern. Load the brush in Antique Gold, sweep through Red Iron Oxide and place in petal 1. Sweep through a little more Red Iron Oxide to darken and place in petal 2.

Wipe the brush on paper towel, sideload in Light Buttermilk and lay down the white along the edge of petal 3. Wipe the brush on paper towel, sweep through Antique Gold and pull the white down. Wipe the brush on paper towel, sideload in Light Buttermilk and lay the white down along the edge of petal 4. Wipe the brush, sweep through Antique Gold and pull the white down. Turn your work upside down and use the liner brush and Red Iron Oxide to pull up fine lines from the near the stem.

Daisies Working one petal at a time, sideload in Light Buttermilk and lay the white down along the edge of the petal. Wipe the brush, sweep through Yellow Ochre and pull the white edge in towards the centre. The upturned profile daisy is painted the same way, but when painting its back petals sweep through a little Yellow Ochre then sweep through a little Red Iron Oxide as well. Hold the Red Iron Oxide to the surface and pull the white edge in towards the centre.

Centres Tap in a circle of Antique Gold and while this is still wet, tap a little Red Iron Oxide along the bottom of the circle and a little Light Buttermilk across the top.

Morning glories Sideload the size 3 brush in Light Buttermilk and lay down the white along the edge of the petals. Wipe the brush on paper towel, sweep through Marigold and pull the white down.

Little daisies Load the brush in Marigold and sweep through Light Buttermilk. Hold the Light Buttermilk to the surface and paint the petals across the back. Sideload in Light Buttermilk and place in the petals across the front with the Light Buttermilk facing in towards the centre. Use light pressure to start off, then increase pressure as you move across and decrease pressure to finish off. Place a Red Iron Oxide dot in the middle with a smaller Light Buttermilk dot on top of that.

Snowdrops Paint a ball of Yellow Ochre. Sideload the dirty brush (keep the Yellow Ochre in the brush—don't wash it out) in Light Buttermilk and paint an S-stroke down either side of the ball with the Light Buttermilk held to the outside of the ball. Sweep through Light Buttermilk and place in the daisy stroke in the middle.

Fuchsia Load the brush in Red Iron Oxide and sweep through Antique Gold. Hold the Antique Gold to the surface and paint the calyx. The fuchsia bud is painted this way as well—just paint two blobs one above the other. Wash the brush, sideload in Light Buttermilk and lay the Light Buttermilk down along the petal line. Wipe the brush, sweep through True Ochre and pull the Light Buttermilk in towards the calyx. Wash the brush, load in Red Iron Oxide, sweep through Antique Gold and with the Antique Gold held towards the surface paint an S-stroke sepal on either side of the calyx. Sweep through a *little* Light Buttermilk and hold this to the surface and paint the middle sepal. Load the liner brush in Red Iron Oxide, sweep through Antique Gold and paint three sit-downs for the stamens.

Native violets (see worksheet on page 38) Load the brush in Red Iron Oxide, sweep through Antique Gold and with the gold held to the surface paint the back petal and the two side petals.

Sweep through a little Light Buttermilk and with this held to the surface place in the front petal. Place a Leaf Mix dot in the centre.

Wash leaves Thin the Leaf Mix with water. Use the size 3 brush to paint in the transparent leaves which are indicated on the pattern by broken lines. Load the brush in the thinned paint, touch the tip on paper towel (this will stop the thinned paint from making a blob on your piece), and use a combination of comma strokes and S-strokes to paint in the leaves.

Paint in the wash leaves around the side of the bowl with the size 3 brush, using the liner brush and the same mix for the stems.

Fillers Load the liner brush in Light Buttermilk and place these in.

Stems and calyces All the stems on the flowers, except the tulip stem, are painted with Leaf Mix using the liner brush. To paint the tulip stem, load the size 3 brush in Leaf Mix and sweep through Antique Gold. Hold the gold to the surface and paint in the stem.

To paint the calyx on the morning glory, load the brush in Leaf Mix, sweep through Antique Gold and with the gold held to the surface paint the two outside S-strokes. Keeping the same brush loading, sweep through a little Light Buttermilk on the gold side and with the Light Buttermilk held to the surface paint the middle calyx.

Antique using Burnt Umber oil paint following the instructions on page 26.

Varnish with your favourite oil-compatible varnish.

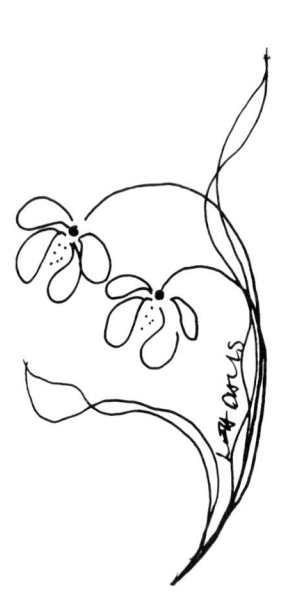

PATTERNS

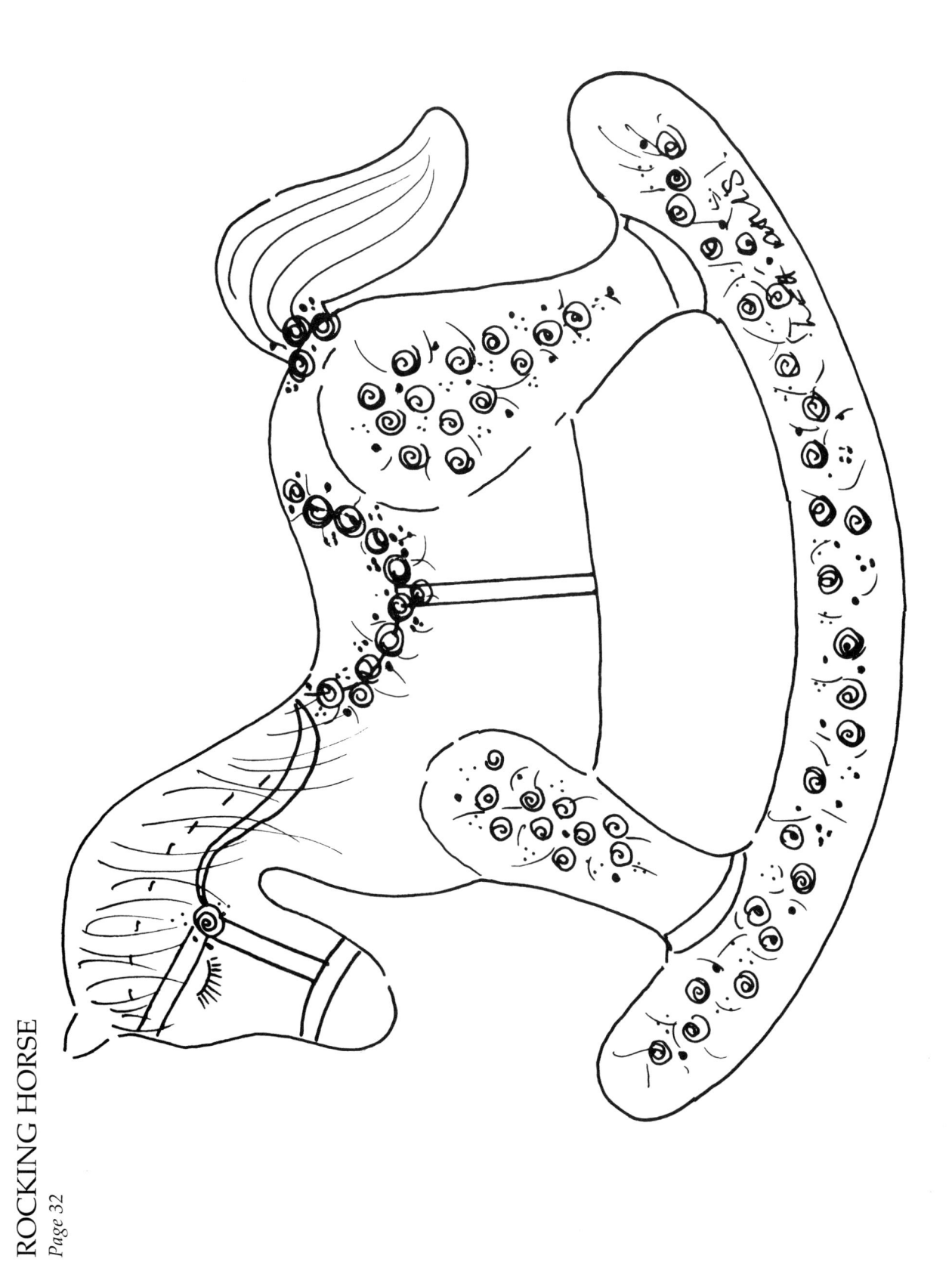

ROCKING HORSE
Page 32

67

OVAL GARLAND BOX
Page 35

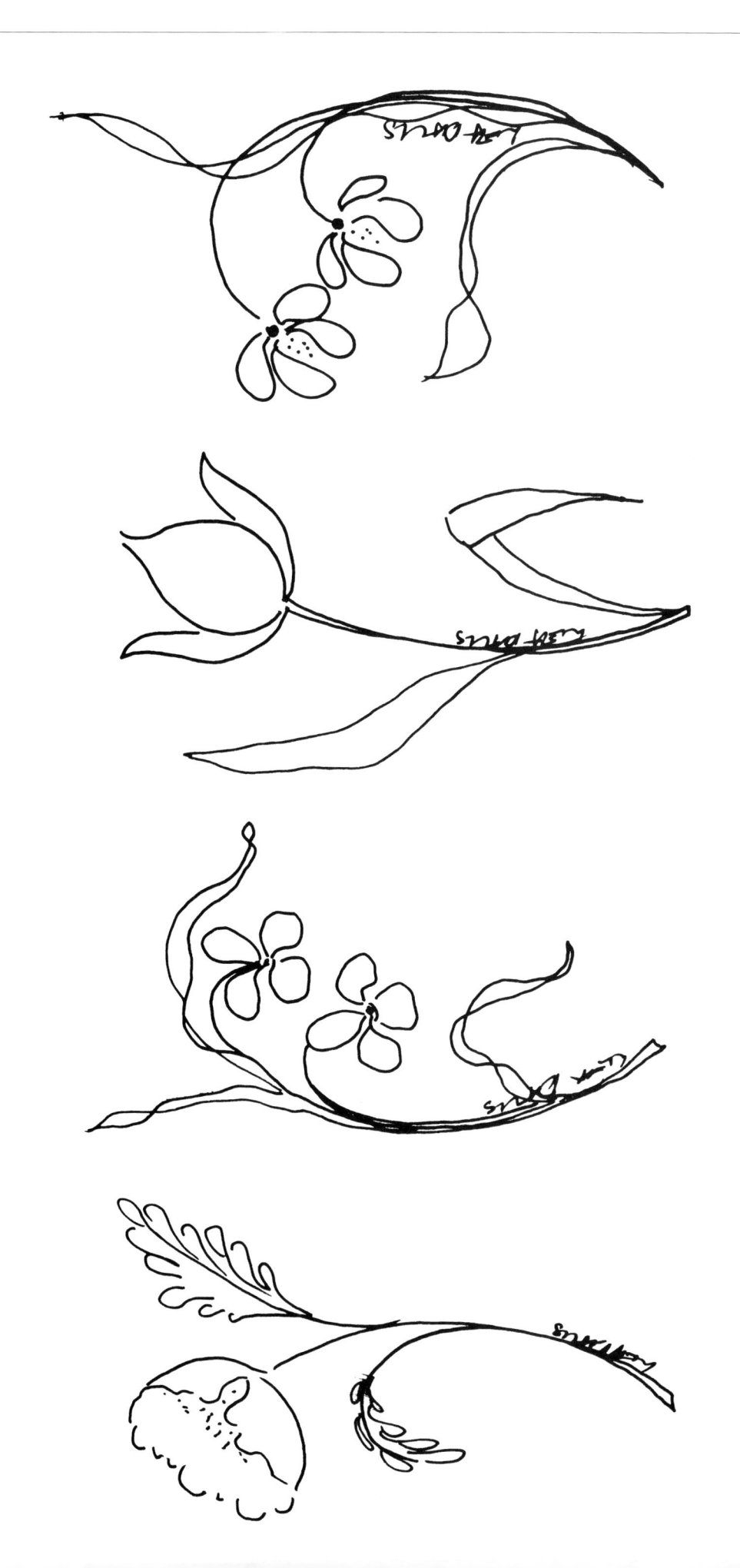

LAP DESK AND PENCIL CADDY SET
Page 37

LAP DESK AND PENCIL CADDY SET
Page 37

GARDEN SET
Page 41

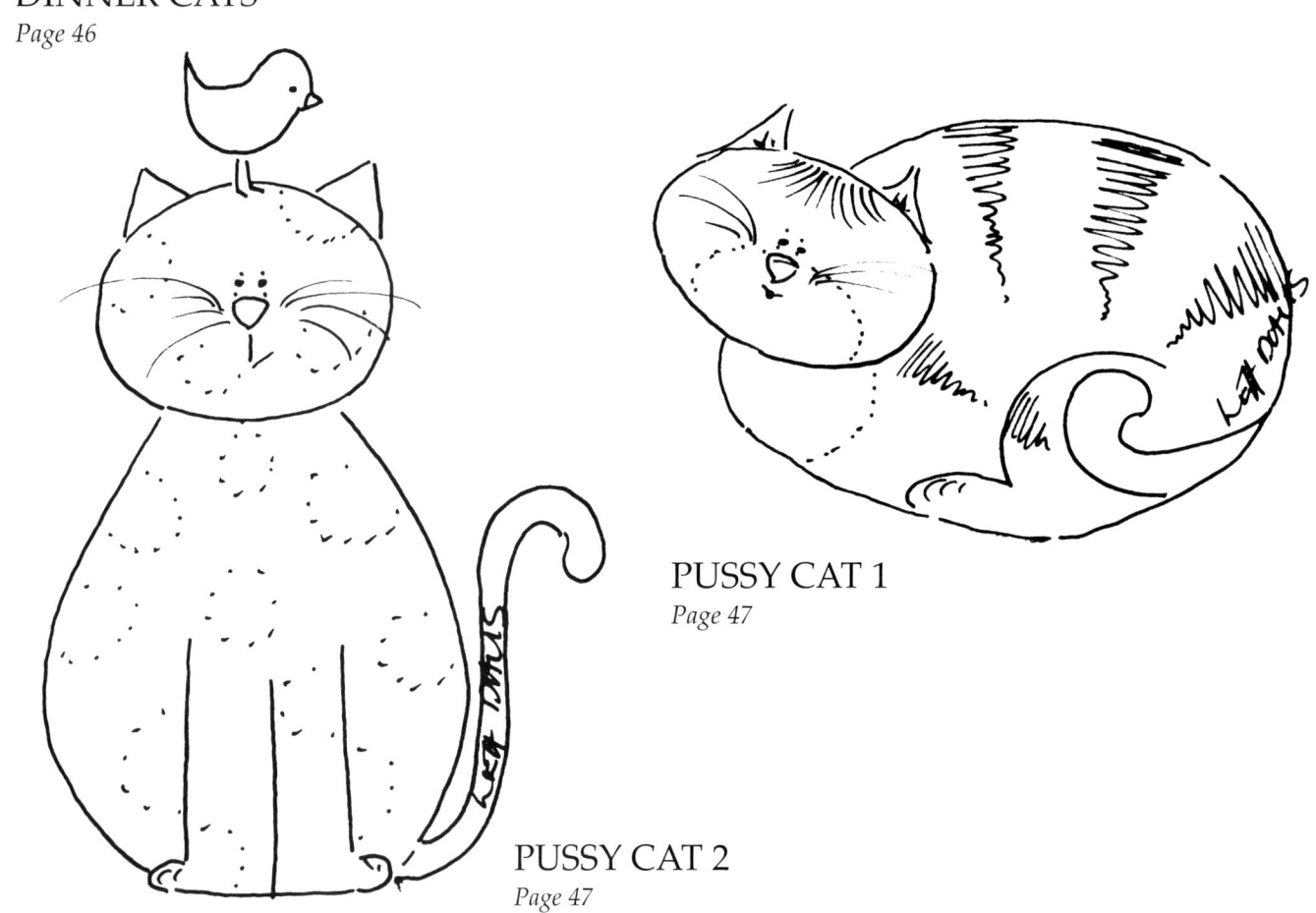

FAUX FINISH COASTER BOX WITH PEONIES
Page 44 (illustrated on page 6)

DINNER CATS
Page 46

PUSSY CAT 1
Page 47

PUSSY CAT 2
Page 47

PUSSY CAT 3
Page 47

PUSSY CAT 6
Page 48

PUSSY CAT 4
Pages 47–48

PUSSY CAT 5
Page 48

PUSSY CAT 10
Page 49

PUSSY CAT 7
Page 48

PUSSY CAT 9
Page 49

PUSSY CAT 8
Page 49

THREE PAPIER-MÂCHÉ DAISY BOXES
Page 50

75

PANSY TEAPOT AND SUGARBOWL
Page 55

ROSES HEART BOX
Page 53

TISSUE BOX
COVER AND
PICTURE
FRAME
Page 58

WILDFLOWER BOX
Page 60

BLUE BOWL
Page 63

79

STOCKISTS

TIMBERTURN P/L (wholesale only)
63 Boothby St
Panorama South Australia 5041
Ph: (08) 8277 5056
Rocking Horse (page 32)

CRAFT TURN
c/o Post Office
Streatham Victoria 3351
Ph: (03) 5350 7655
Oval Garland Box (page 35), Faux Finish Coaster Box (page 44), Blue Bowl (page 63)

TECO HANDCRAFTS
PO Box 403
Kyneton Victoria 3444
Ph: (03) 5424 8488
Lap Desk and Pencil Caddy (page 7), Roses Heart Box (page 53), Wildflower Box (page 60)

WALLA WALLA WOODCRAFT
3 Victoria St
Walla Walla NSW 2659
Ph: (02) 6029 2409
Pansy Teapot and Sugar Bowl (page 55), Tissue Box Cover and Frame (page 58)

FOSs AUSTRALASIA P/L (wholesale only)
14 Hardner Rd
Mt Waverly
Ph: (03) 9543 5533
Dinner Cats (page 46)

AUSTRALIAN CRAFT DISTRIBUTORS
51 Seymour St
Ringwood Victoria 3134
Ph: (03) 9870 4522
Papier-mâché Boxes (page 50)

INDEX

Basecoating 12
Basic equipment 9
Blooming 29
Bristle brush 8
Brush stroke worksheet 16
Brushes 8
C-stroke (round brush) 17
Caring for your brushes 8
Chezza-B palette 9
Cleaning your brushes 9
Comma stroke (liner brush) 17
Crackling 30
Criss-cross background technique 25
Cross-hatching 18
Daisy stroke (round brush) 15
Dots 22
Dressing the brush 14
Dutch metal 27
Faux finish 23
French craqueler 30
Gilding 27
Hand and body position 14
Lea Davis brush set 10
Mop brush 27
Oil antiquing 26

Paints 8
Palette 9
Pre-mixed stains 30
Pull-in 21
S-stroke (liner brush) 17
S-stroke (round brush) 15
Sandwich crackle 30
Selective antiquing 27
Sideloading (round brush) 19
Skewings 28
Sponge brush 12
Sponging 23
Staining 29
Stroke formation 14
Surface preparation 11
Sweeping 22
Swirls and tendrils 18
Teardrops 17
Tipping 22
Top coat crackle 30
Tracing the design 13
Transferring the design 13
Varnishing 29
Water-based antiquing 27
Wax 29